PRAGMATISM
AND AMERICAN CULTURE

Problems in American Civilization

READINGS SELECTED BY THE
DEPARTMENT OF AMERICAN STUDIES
AMHERST COLLEGE

Puritanism in Early America

The Causes of the American Revolution

The Declaration of Independence and the Constitution

Hamilton and the National Debt

The Turner Thesis concerning the Role of the Frontier in American History

Jackson versus Biddle — The Struggle over the Second Bank of the United States

The Transcendentalist Revolt against Materialism

Slavery as a Cause of the Civil War

Democracy and the Gospel of Wealth

John D. Rockefeller — Robber Baron or Industrial Statesman?

Roosevelt, Wilson, and the Trusts

Pragmatism and American Culture

The New Deal — Revolution or Evolution?

Industry-wide Collective Bargaining — Promise or Menace?

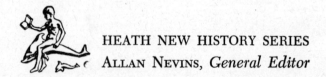

HEATH NEW HISTORY SERIES

ALLAN NEVINS, *General Editor*

PRAGMATISM and
AMERICAN CULTURE

EDITED WITH AN INTRODUCTION BY

Gail Kennedy

Problems in American Civilization

READINGS SELECTED BY THE
DEPARTMENT OF AMERICAN STUDIES
AMHERST COLLEGE

D. C. HEATH AND COMPANY: Boston

INTRODUCTION

IN 1778 the French statesman Turgot wrote of the Americans:

This people is the hope of the human race. It may become the model. It ought to show the world by facts, that men can be free and yet peaceful, and may dispense with the chains in which tyrants and knaves of every colour have presumed to bind them, under pretext of the public good. The Americans should be an example of political, religious, commercial and industrial liberty.

For Turgot the American Revolution opened a new chapter in human history, because America was the first society explicitly founded upon a philosophy of liberty. That philosophy was expressed in the Declaration of Independence. And the rights and freedoms which Jefferson had declared in the eighteenth century were reaffirmed in their separate ways by Emerson and Whitman during the middle period of our history. These men were the philosophers of American democracy.

The only obvious successor in our day to the philosophies of Jefferson and Emerson and Whitman is the "pragmatism" of William James and John Dewey. All of the critics from whose writings selections have been made for this volume agree that Pragmatism is an indigenous American philosophy; most of them would add that it is *the* philosophy which best expresses the "climate of opinion" peculiar to American civilization. Their criticisms, therefore, take two forms: they may argue that, granted *pragmatism* is a native philosophy, it is but a partial and inadequate representation of certain trends within our culture; or they may contend that pragmatism is only too faithful a transcription of American life. Critics of the first sort will disparage those particular traits of our society which they think pragmatism represents; critics of the second kind will deliver a wholesale condemnation of "Americanism." In effect, therefore, all of these writers in their discussions of the pragmatic philosophy are censuring what is distinctive of American culture itself, in some of its aspects or as a whole.

The critics from whose writings a selection has been made for this volume, though there are some interesting points of agreement among them, represent four distinct groups: Lewis Mumford speaks for a set of literary critics and publicists, such men as Randolph Bourne, Waldo Frank and Van Wyck Brooks, authors who have similar opinions about "pragmatic America"; Reinhold Niebuhr writes from the viewpoint of that form of Protestant Christianity known as "neo-orthodoxy"; Mortimer J. Adler is a Thomist, though not a Catholic; and Howard Selsam states the Marxist position.

The first selection, chapters one and two of James' *Pragmatism* (1907), gives in his inimitably fresh and vigorous style a characterization of the pragmatic attitude towards philosophical problems and a definition of pragmatism as a method. The pragmatic attitude he characterizes as one "of looking away from first things, principles, 'categories,' supposed necessities; and of looking towards last things, fruits, consequences, facts." Although James put as subtitle to his volume "A New Name for Some Old Ways of Thinking," the pragmatic method was far more original than his modesty would allow him to profess. Most of the great turning points in thought have been revolutions in method. James was conscious of this; in a letter to his brother, written just as he had finished the proofs, he said of the book, "I shouldn't be surprised if ten years hence it should be rated as 'epoch-making,' for of the definitive triumph of that general way of thinking I can entertain no doubt whatever — I believe it to be something quite like the protestant reformation."

Though deeply interested in social questions, James was preoccupied with the application of the new method to more general philosophical problems and to certain topics in the field of morals and religion. It remained for Dewey to use the method for the working out of a comprehensive social theory. The second selection consists of a brief summary by Dewey of his philosophy, "What I Believe," published in *The Forum* (1930) as one of "A Series of Intimate Credos," together with a reconsideration of this statement written ten years later. Dewey here affirms his faith that "a thorough-going philosophy of experience, framed in the light of science and technique," can provide the basis for the dynamic idealism implicit in American democracy.

The next part of the readings gives, under the title "The Pragmatic Acquiescence," Lewis Mumford's criticism of James and Dewey in his book, *The Golden Day* (1926), Dewey's reply, and the brief rejoinder by Mumford which terminates the controversy. Mumford contends that William James "was only warming over again in philosophy the hash of everyday experience in the Gilded Age"; he even "gave this attitude of compromise and acquiescence a name; he called it pragmatism." And Dewey, he charges, has bestowed a similar benediction on our own generation. Mumford feels that Randolph Bourne "put his finger upon the shallow side of Mr. Dewey's thinking" when he stated that the practical effect of his philosophy was to subordinate ends to means, vision to technique. In the next item, the essay entitled "Pragmatic America" (1922), Dewey comments on the similar criticism advanced by Bertrand Russell:

The two qualities which I consider superlatively important are love of truth and love of our neighbor. I find love of truth in America obscured by commercialism of which pragmatism is the philosophical expression; and love of our neighbor kept in fetters by Puritan morality.

Reinhold Niebuhr and Mortimer Adler, as critics of pragmatism from the standpoint of orthodox types of religion, have one basic intent in common: pragmatism they condemn as an attempt to set up the cult of science as a new means of salvation. Niebuhr, in the preface to *Moral Man and Immoral Society* (1930), makes the point that the development of scientifically experimental procedures for the purposeful control of social changes is impossible in a community where there are "dominant social classes who are trying to maintain their special privileges in society." These pragmatic moralists fail to realize the "stubborn resistance of group egoism to all moral and inclusive social objectives." Niebuhr's conclusion, a conclusion in which he is diametrically opposed to the Marxists, is that "man's collective behavior will never be conquered by reason, unless reason uses tools, and is itself driven by forces that are not rational." These "forces" are, of course, those of religious faith in a supernatural order to whose purposes the realm of nature is subordinate.

Mortimer Adler's "God and the Professors" is an address delivered in 1940 at the first of a series of annual conferences on science, philosophy and religion in their relation to the democratic way of life. It is a broadside attack upon the "professors." "The defects of modern culture," says Professor Adler, "are the defects of its intellectual leaders, its teachers and savants." Despite the vast diversity of their particular opinions, most of them, he asserts, are positivists. Thus "behind the multiplicity of technical jargons there is a single doctrine. The essential point of that doctrine is simply the affirmation of science, and the denial of philosophy and religion." The "most serious threat to Democracy is the positivism of the professors, which dominates every aspect of modern education and is the central corruption of modern culture." While Professor Adler does not in this address name names, the pragmatists are clearly foremost among those he means. In an essay, "This Pre-War Generation," published in *Harper's* that same year, he specifically declares that it is "corrupt pragmatic liberalism," the "kind denounced by Lewis Mumford," which is the source of our demoralization. In the next selection, a brief article entitled *The New Medievalism*, Sidney Hook, one of the leading younger pragmatists, replies to Adler. Professor Hook particularly resents Adler's charge that "Democracy has much more to fear from the mentality of its teachers than from the nihilism of Hitler." Hook retorts that it is not the socially cooperative method of enquiry we call "scientific" but Professor Adler's intolerant and dogmatic assertions that invite comparisons with the mentality of Hitler.

The Marxist line of criticism is the final one here presented. Howard Selsam in these excerpts from his book, *Socialism and Ethics* (1943), contends, in agreement with Reinhold Niebuhr, that ours is a society characterized by conflicting class interests; and he agrees with Niebuhr that in such a situation the experimental methods of science cannot be applied to social problems. But from this common basis of agreement he draws a radically divergent conclusion. The scientific attitude involves values, he argues, which are identical with the interests of certain of those classes, "those classes and groups whose needs are harmonious with, and require the fuller development of, our productive forces." What the pragmatists preach but can never put into practice is a "pseudo-science that categorically eliminates from the picture the actual nature of men and of existing social forces." The "inadequacy and subtly reactionary nature" of this approach is "tantamount to the denial of class conflict and of irreconcilable social forces. Thus it affirms the basic rationality of the capitalist order."

The next selection is a short essay by Sidney Hook, "John Dewey and His Critics" (1931), which serves here as a summing up of the pragmatist's reply to the various sorts of criticism that have been advanced. In particular, Professor Hook attempts to meet the recurrent charge of these critics, that "Dewey tells us how to get ten steps ahead, but he does not tell us, where and what the goal is."

In the final selection, the third chapter of *Liberalism and Social Action* (1935), Dewey is given the last word. Here he describes in more detail what he means by the application of scientific methods of enquiry as a means of analyzing and dealing with social problems. Here, also, he replies in detail to the objection that vested interests and class antagonisms will effectually prevent the use of the methods of intelligence. In this connection, he criticizes, in contrast with his own view, the Marxist theory of social change.

Jefferson, Emerson, and Whitman addressed a brave, new world. Today, however, the confident optimism of their voices sounds thin and hollow to many ears. We live in an age of anxiety, one in which the presumption is current that liberalism is dead. Even so robust a defender of the faith as Arthur M. Schlesinger, Jr., can say casually, almost as though it were axiomatic, "A time of perplexity creates a need for somber and tragic interpretations of man. Thus we find Burke more satisfying today than Paine, Hamilton or Adams than Jefferson, Calhoun than Webster or Clay."[1] And Reinhold Niebuhr in his recent book, *Faith and History,* quotes with the air of one vindicated the final confession of H. G. Wells, leading apostle of Western progress:

A frightful queerness has come into life. Hitherto events have been held together by a certain logical consistency as the heavenly bodies have been held together by the golden cord of gravitation. Now it is as if the cord had vanished and everything is driven anyhow, anywhere at a steadily increasing velocity. . . . The writer is convinced that there is no way out, or around, or through the impasse. It is the end.

On this Niebuhr comments: "The spiritual pilgrimage of Mr. Wells is an almost perfect record in miniature of the spiritual pilgrimage of our age."

The cause of this anxiety and despair

[1] *The Nation,* April 1, 1950, p. 302.

is only too obvious, it stems from man's uneasy consciousness that he now holds within his power the means of his own destruction. That this power is also the means of realizing the hopes of Turgot — and of H. G. Wells — seems to an increasing number utopian — utopian because the world they have known is one of global wars and depression, one in which the defeat of fascism was only followed by the coalescence of world power into two rival centers that cannot be reconciled.

One of these centers exemplifies the effects that a philosophy can exert when it inspires and is diffused throughout an entire culture. "The philosophers," said Marx, "have only *interpreted* the world in various ways, the point, however, is to *change* it." Dialectical materialism has provided an interpretation of the world that *is* changing it. Communism is a definitely articulated creed which has all the moving force of a world religion. The philosophy behind the American democracy of the eighteenth century likewise transformed *its* world. In this debate over pragmatism, American civilization itself is on trial. Is the pragmatic philosophy a misleading and perverted justification of the worst elements in a "business civilization"? Or is it an authentic expression of the dynamic idealism of "the American way of life"? If there is a "challenge of communism," this is one of its most fundamental aspects.

[NOTE: The statements on page x are quoted, with the permission of the publishers, from the following sources: Lloyd Morris, *Postscript to Yesterday* (New York: Random House, 1947), pp. 368–369; Mortimer J. Adler, "This Pre-War Generation," *Harper's Magazine,* Vol. 181 (October, 1940), 527; M. Dynnik, "Contemporary Bourgeois Philosophy in the U.S.," *Modern Review,* I, No. 9 (November, 1947), 658; John Dewey, *Liberalism and Social Action* (New York: G. P. Putnam's Sons, 1935), pp. 91–92.]

CONTENTS

The Clash of Issues

A historian frames the question:

"By the mid-nineteen forties, pragmatism had touched the lives of two generations of Americans. Perhaps never before had a philosophy been applied so hopefully, over so wide an area, to shape the minds of youth to the uses of a greater freedom. If social power and insight were developed in the young, must not society eventually be perfected? Whether or not they knew it, most Americans born in the twentieth century played some part in this experiment. For it had taken place in the most universal of their institutions. In less than fifty years, pragmatism had transformed the American school."

— Lloyd Morris

A Thomist philosopher answers:

". . . . The very things which constituted the cultural departure that we call modern times have eventuated, not only in the perverted education of American youth to-day, but also in the crises they are unprepared to face. That fascism should have reached its stride in Europe at the same time that pseudo-liberalism — the kind Lewis Mumford denounces as corrupt, pragmatic liberalism — has demoralized us, is an historic accident. Only the timing is a coincidence, however, for both the European and the American maladies arise from the same causes. They are both the last fruitions of modern man's exclusive trust in science and his gradual disavowal of whatever lies beyond the field of science as irrational prejudice, as opinion emotionally held."

— Mortimer J. Adler

While a Bolshevik charges:

"The philosophy of pragmatism is a philosophy of active service to American reaction. Preaching the idea of "harmony" between the exploiters and the exploited, bedeviling the consciousness of the masses with a business psychology, paving the way for clericalism, reactionary pragmatism strives to penetrate among the working classes in order to corrupt them spiritually and subject them to the influence of bourgeois ideology."

— M. Dynnik

And John Dewey reaffirms his belief:

". . . . Democracy has been a fighting faith. When its ideals are reenforced by those of scientific method and experimental intelligence, it cannot be that it is incapable of evoking discipline, ardor and organization. . . . I for one do not believe that Americans living in the tradition of Jefferson and Lincoln will weaken and give up without a whole-hearted effort to make democracy a living reality."

William James: WHAT PRAGMATISM MEANS

The Present Dilemma in Philosophy

IN the preface to that admirable collection of essays of his called 'Heretics,' Mr. Chesterton writes these words: "There are some people — and I am one of them — who think that the most practical and important thing about a man is still his view of the universe. We think that for a landlady considering a lodger it is important to know his income, but still more important to know his philosophy. We think that for a general about to fight an enemy it is important to know the enemy's numbers, but still more important to know the enemy's philosophy. We think the question is not whether the theory of the cosmos affects matters, but whether in the long run anything else affects them."

I think with Mr. Chesterton in this matter. I know that you, ladies and gentlemen, have a philosophy, each and all of you, and that the most interesting and important thing about you is the way in which it determines the perspective in your several worlds. You know the same of me. And yet I confess to a certain tremor at the audacity of the enterprise which I am about to begin. For the philosophy which is so important in each of us is not a technical matter; it is our more or less dumb sense of what life honestly and deeply means. It is only partly got from books; it is our individual way of just seeing and feeling the total push and pressure of the cosmos. I have no right to assume that many of you are students of the cosmos in the classroom sense, yet here I stand desirous of interesting you in a philosophy which to no small extent has to be technically treated. I wish to fill you with sympathy with a contemporaneous tendency in which I profoundly believe, and yet I have to talk like a professor to you who are not students. Whatever universe a professor believes in must at any rate be a universe that lends itself to lengthy discourse. A universe definable in two sentences is something for which the professorial intellect has no use. No faith in anything of that cheap kind! I have heard friends and colleagues try to popularize philosophy in this very hall, but they soon grew dry, and then technical, and the results were only partially encouraging. So my enterprise is a bold one. The founder of pragmatism himself recently gave a course of lectures at the Lowell Institute with that very word in its title, — flashes of brilliant light relieved against Cimmerian darkness! None of us, I fancy, understood all that he said — yet here I stand, making a very similar venture.

I risk it because the very lectures I speak of drew — they brought good audiences. There is, it must be confessed, a curious fascination in hearing deep things talked about, even though neither we nor the disputants understand them. We get the problematic thrill, we feel the presence of the vastness. Let a controversy begin in a smoking-room anywhere, about free-will or God's omniscience, or good and evil, and see how every one in the place pricks up his ears. Philosophy's results concern us all most vitally, and philosophy's queerest arguments tickle agreeably our sense of subtlety and ingenuity.

Believing in philosophy myself devoutly, and believing also that a kind of new dawn is breaking upon us philosophers, I feel impelled, *per fas aut nefas*, to try to impart to you some news of the situation.

Philosophy is at once the most sublime and the most trivial of human pursuits. It works in the minutest crannies and it opens out the widest vistas. It 'bakes no bread,' as has been said, but it can inspire our souls with courage; and repugnant as its manners, its doubting and challenging, its quibbling and dialectics, often are to common people, no one of us can get along without the far-flashing beams of light it sends over the world's perspectives. These illuminations at least, and the contrast-effects of darkness and mystery that accompany them, give to what it says an interest that is much more than professional.

The history of philosophy is to a great extent that of a certain clash of human temperaments. Undignified as such a treatment may seem to some of my colleagues, I shall have to take account of this clash and explain a good many of the divergencies of philosophers by it. Of whatever temperament a professional philosopher is, he tries, when philosophizing, to sink the fact of his temperament. Temperament is no conventionally recognized reason, so he urges impersonal reasons only for his conclusions. Yet his temperament really gives him a stronger bias than any of his more strictly objective premises. It loads the evidence for him one way or the other, making for a more sentimental or a more hardhearted view of the universe, just as this fact or that principle would. He *trusts* his temperament. Wanting a universe

that suits it, he believes in any representation of the universe that does suit it. He feels men of opposite temper to be out of key with the world's character, and in his heart considers them incompetent and 'not in it,' in the philosophic business, even though they may far excel him in dialectical ability.

Yet in the forum he can make no claim, on the bare ground of his temperament, to superior discernment or authority. There arises thus a certain insincerity in our philosophic discussions: the potentest of all our premises is never mentioned. I am sure it would contribute to clearness if in these lectures we should break this rule and mention it, and I accordingly feel free to do so.

Of course I am talking here of very positively marked men, men of radical idiosyncrasy, who have set their stamp and likeness on philosophy and figure in its history. Plato, Locke, Hegel, Spencer, are such temperamental thinkers. Most of us have, of course, no very definite intellectual temperament, we are a mixture of opposite ingredients, each one present very moderately. We hardly know our own preferences in abstract matters; some of us are easily talked out of them, and end by following the fashion or taking up with the beliefs of the most impressive philosopher in our neighborhood, whoever he may be. But the one thing that has *counted* so far in philosophy is that a man should *see* things, see them straight in his own peculiar way, and be dissatisfied with any opposite way of seeing them. There is no reason to suppose that this strong temperamental vision is from now onward to count no longer in the history of man's beliefs.

Now the particular difference of temperament that I have in mind in making these remarks is one that has counted in literature, art, government, and manners as well as in philosophy. In manners we find formalists and free-and-easy persons. In government, authoritarians and anarchists. In literature, purists or academicals, and realists. In art, classics and romantics. You recognize these contrasts as familiar; well, in philosophy we have a very similar contrast expressed in the pair of terms 'rationalist' and 'empiricist,' 'empiricist' meaning your lover of facts in all their crude variety, 'rationalist' meaning your devotee to abstract and eternal principles. No one can live an hour without both facts and principles, so it is a difference rather of emphasis; yet it breeds antipathies of the most pungent character between those who lay the emphasis differently; and we shall find it extraordinarily convenient to express a certain contrast in men's ways of taking their universe, by talking of the 'empiricist' and of the 'rationalist' temper. These terms make the contrast simple and massive.

More simple and massive than are usually the men of whom the terms are predicated. For every sort of permutation and combination is possible in human nature; and if I now proceed to define more fully what I have in mind when I speak of rationalists and empiricists, by adding to each of those titles some secondary qualifying characteristics, I beg you to regard my conduct as to a certain extent arbitrary. I select types of combination that nature offers very frequently, but by no means uniformly, and I select them solely for their convenience in helping me to my ulterior purpose of characterizing pragmatism. Historically we find the terms 'intellectualism' and 'sensationalism' used as synonyms of 'rationalism' and 'empiricism.' Well, nature seems to combine most frequently with intellectualism an idealistic and optimistic tendency. Empiricists on the other hand are not uncommonly materialistic, and their optimism is apt to be decidedly conditional and tremulous. Rationalism is always monistic. It starts from wholes and universals, and makes much of the unity of things. Empiricism starts from the parts, and makes of the whole a collection — is not averse therefore to calling itself pluralistic. Rationalism usually considers itself more religious than empiricism, but there is much to say about this claim, so I merely mention it. It is a true claim when the individual rationalist is what is called a man of feeling, and when the individual empiricist prides himself on being hard-headed. In that case the rationalist will usually also be in favor of what is called free-will, and the empiricist will be a fatalist — I use the terms most popularly current. The rationalist finally will be of dogmatic temper in his affirmations, while the empiricist may be more sceptical and open to discussion.

I will write these traits down in two columns. I think you will practically recognize the two types of mental make-up that I mean if I head the columns by the titles 'tender-minded' and 'tough-minded' respectively.

THE TENDER-MINDED.	THE TOUGH-MINDED.
Rationalistic (going by 'principles'),	Empiricist (going by 'facts'),
Intellectualistic,	Sensationalistic,
Idealistic,	Materialistic,
Optimistic,	Pessimistic,
Religious,	Irreligious,
Free-willist,	Fatalistic,
Monistic,	Pluralistic,
Dogmatical.	Sceptical.

Pray postpone for a moment the question whether the two contrasted mixtures which I have written down are each inwardly coherent and self-consistent or not — I shall very soon have a good deal to say on that point. It suffices for our immediate purpose that tender-minded and tough-minded people, characterized as I have written them down, do both exist. Each of you probably knows some well-marked example of each type, and you know what each example thinks of the example on the other side of the line. They have a low opinion of each other. Their antagonism, whenever as individuals their temperaments have been intense, has formed in all ages a part of the philosophic atmosphere of the time. It forms a part of the philosophic atmosphere to-day. The tough think of the tender as sentimentalists and soft-heads. The tender feel the tough to be unrefined, callous, or brutal. Their mutual reaction is very much like that that takes place when Bostonian tourists mingle with a population like that of Cripple Creek. Each type believes the other to be inferior to itself; but disdain in the one case is mingled with amusement, in the other it has a dash of fear.

Now, as I have already insisted, few of us are tender-foot Bostonians pure and simple, and few are typical Rocky Mountain toughs, in philosophy. Most of us have a hankering for the good things on both sides of the line. Facts are good, of course — give us lots of facts. Principles are good — give us plenty of principles. The world is indubitably one if you look at it in one way, but as indubitably is it many, if you look at it in another. It is both one and many — let us adopt a sort of pluralistic monism. Everything of course is necessarily determined, and yet of course our wills are free: a sort of free-will determinism is the true philosophy. The evil of the parts is undeniable, but the whole can't be evil: so practical pessimism may be combined with meta-physical optimism. And so forth — your ordinary philosophic layman never being a radical, never straightening out his system, but living vaguely in one plausible compartment of it or another to suit the temptations of successive hours.

But some of us are more than mere laymen in philosophy. We are worthy of the name of amateur athletes, and are vexed by too much inconsistency and vacillation in our creed. We cannot preserve a good intellectual conscience so long as we keep mixing incompatibles from opposite sides of the line.

And now I come to the first positively important point which I wish to make. Never were as many men of a decidedly empiricist proclivity in existence as there are at the present day. Our children, one may say, are almost born scientific. But our esteem for facts has not neutralized in us all religiousness. It is itself almost religious. Our scientific temper is devout. Now take a man of this type, and let him be also a philosophic amateur, unwilling to mix a hodge-podge system after the fashion of a common layman, and what does he find his situation to be, in this blessed year of our Lord 1906? He wants facts; he wants science; but he also wants a religion. And being an amateur and not an independent originator in philosophy he naturally looks for guidance to the experts and professionals whom he finds already in the field. A very large number of you here present, possibly a majority of you, are amateurs of just this sort.

Now what kinds of philosophy do you find actually offered to meet your need? You find an empirical philosophy that is not religious enough, and a religious philosophy that is not empirical enough for your purpose. If you look to the quarter where facts are most considered you find the whole tough-minded program in operation, and the 'conflict between science and religion' in full blast. Either it is that Rocky Mountain tough of a Haeckel with his materialistic monism, his ether-god and his jest at your God as a 'gaseous vertebrate'; or it is Spencer treating the world's history as a redistribution of matter and motion solely, and bowing religion politely out at the front door: — she may indeed continue to exist, but she must never show her face inside the temple.

For a hundred and fifty years past the progress of science has seemed to mean the enlargement of the material universe and the diminution of man's importance. The result is what one may call the growth of naturalistic or positivistic feeling. Man is no lawgiver to nature, he is an absorber. She it is who stands firm; he it is who must accommodate himself. Let him record truth, inhuman though it be, and submit to it! The romantic spontaneity and courage are gone, the vision is materialistic and depressing. Ideals appear as inert by-products of physiology; what is higher is explained by what is lower and treated forever as a case of 'nothing but' — nothing but something else of a quite inferior sort. You get, in short, a materialistic universe, in which only the tough-minded find themselves congenially at home.

If now, on the other hand, you turn to the religious quarter for consolation, and take counsel of the tender-minded philosophies, what do you find?

Religious philosophy in our day and generation is, among us English-reading people, of two main types. One of these is more radical and aggressive, the other has more the air of fighting a slow retreat. By the more radical wing of religious philosophy I mean the so-called transcendental idealism of the Anglo-Hegelian school, the philosophy of such men as Green, the Cairds, Bosanquet, and Royce. This philosophy has greatly influenced the more studious members of our protestant ministry. It is pantheistic, and undoubtedly it has already blunted the edge of the traditional theism in protestantism at large.

That theism remains, however. It is the lineal descendant, through one stage of concession after another, of the dogmatic scholastic theism still taught rigorously in the seminaries of the catholic church. For a long time it used to be called among us the philosophy of the Scottish school. It is what I meant by the philosophy that has the air of fighting a slow retreat. Between the encroachments of the hegelians and other philosophers of the 'Absolute,' on the one hand, and those of the scientific evolutionists and agnostics, on the other, the men that give us this kind of a philosophy, James Martineau, Professor Bowne, Professor Ladd and others, must feel themselves rather tightly squeezed. Fair-minded and candid as you like, this philosophy is not radical in temper. It is eclectic, a thing of compromises, that seeks a *modus vivendi* above all things. It accepts the facts of Darwinism, the facts of cerebral physiology, but it does nothing active or enthusiastic with them. It lacks the victorious and aggressive note. It lacks *prestige* in consequence; whereas absolutism has a certain prestige due to the more radical style of it.

These two systems are what you have to choose between if you turn to the tender-minded school. And if you are the lovers of facts I have supposed you to be, you find the trail of the serpent of rationalism, of intellectualism, over everything that lies on that side of the line. You escape indeed the materialism that goes with the reigning empiricism; but you pay for your escape by losing contact with the concrete parts of life. The more absolutistic philosophers dwell on so high a level of abstraction that they never even try to come down. The absolute mind which they offer us, the mind that makes our universe by thinking it, might, for aught they show us to the contrary, have made any one of a million other universes just as well as this. You can deduce no single actual particular from the notion of it. It is compatible with any state of things whatever being true here below. And the theistic God is almost as sterile a principle. You have to go to the world which he has created to get any inkling of his actual character: he is the kind of god that has once for all made that kind of a world. The God of the theistic writers lives on as purely abstract heights as does the Absolute. Absolutism has a certain sweep and dash about it, while the usual theism is more insipid, but both are equally remote and vacuous. What *you* want is a philosophy that will not only exercise your powers of intellectual abstraction, but that will make some positive connexion with this actual world of finite human lives.

You want a system that will combine both things, the scientific loyalty to facts and willingness to take account of them, the spirit of adaptation and accommodation, in short, but also the old confidence in human values and the resultant spontaneity, whether of the religious or of the romantic type. And this is then your dilemma: you find the two parts of your *quaesitum* hopelessly separated. You find empiricism with inhumanism and irreligion; or else you find a rationalistic philosophy that indeed may call itself religious, but that keeps out of all definite touch with concrete facts and joys and sorrows.

I am not sure how many of you live close enough to philosophy to realize

fully what I mean by this last reproach, so I will dwell a little longer on that unreality in all rationalistic systems by which your serious believer in facts is so apt to feel repelled.

I wish that I had saved the first couple of pages of a thesis which a student handed me a year or two ago. They illustrated my point so clearly that I am sorry I can not read them to you now. This young man, who was a graduate of some Western college, began by saying that he had always taken for granted that when you entered a philosophic classroom you had to open relations with a universe entirely distinct from the one you left behind you in the street. The two were supposed, he said, to have so little to do with each other, that you could not possibly occupy your mind with them at the same time. The world of concrete personal experiences to which the street belongs is multitudinous beyond imagination, tangled, muddy, painful and perplexed. The world to which your philosophy-professor introduces you is simple, clean and noble. The contradictions of real life are absent from it. Its architecture is classic. Principles of reason trace its outlines, logical necessities cement its parts. Purity and dignity are what it most expresses. It is a kind of marble temple shining on a hill.

In point of fact it is far less an account of this actual world than a clear addition built upon it, a classic sanctuary in which the rationalist fancy may take refuge from the intolerably confused and gothic character which mere facts present. It is no *explanation* of our concrete universe, it is another thing altogether, a substitute for it, a remedy, a way of escape.

Its temperament, if I may use the word temperament here, is utterly alien to the temperament of existence in the concrete. *Refinement* is what characterizes our intellectualist philosophies. They exquisitely satisfy that craving for a refined object of contemplation which is so powerful an appetite of the mind. But I ask you in all seriousness to look abroad on this colossal universe of concrete facts, on their awful bewilderments, their surprises and cruelties, on the wildness which they show, and then to tell me whether 'refined' is the one inevitable descriptive adjective that springs to your lips.

Refinement has its place in things, true enough. But a philosophy that breathes out nothing but refinement will never satisfy the empiricist temper of mind. It will seem rather a monument of artificiality. So we find men of science preferring to turn their backs on metaphysics as on something altogether cloistered and spectral, and practical men shaking philosophy's dust off their feet and following the call of the wild.

Truly there is something a little ghastly in the satisfaction with which a pure but unreal system will fill a rationalist mind. Leibnitz was a rationalist mind, with infinitely more interest in facts than most rationalist minds can show. Yet if you wish for superficiality incarnate, you have only to read that charmingly written 'Théodicée' of his, in which he sought to justify the ways of God to man, and to prove that the world we live in is the best of possible worlds. Let me quote a specimen of what I mean.

Among other obstacles to his optimistic philosophy, it falls to Leibnitz to consider the number of the eternally damned. That it is infinitely greater, in our human case, than that of those saved, he assumes as a premise from the theologians, and then proceeds to argue in this way. Even then, he says:

The evil will appear as almost nothing in comparison with the good, if we once consider the real magnitude of the City of God.

Coelius Secundus Curio has written a little book, 'De Amplitudine Regni Coelestis,' which was reprinted not long ago. But he failed to compass the extent of the kingdom of the heavens. The ancients had small ideas of the works of God. . . . It seemed to them that only our earth had inhabitants, and even the notion of our antipodes gave them pause. The rest of the world for them consisted of some shining globes and a few crystalline spheres. But to-day, whatever be the limits that we may grant or refuse to the Universe we must recognize in it a countless number of globes, as big as ours or bigger, which have just as much right as it has to support rational inhabitants, tho it does not follow that these need all be men. Our earth is only one among the six principal satellites of our sun. As all the fixed stars are suns, one sees how small a place among visible things our earth takes up, since it is only a satellite of one among them. Now all these suns *may* be inhabited by none but happy creatures; and nothing obliges us to believe that the number of damned persons is very great; for a *very few instances and samples suffice for the utility which good draws from evil*. Moreover, since there is no reason to suppose that there are stars everywhere, may there not be a great space beyond the region of the stars? And this immense space, surrounding all this region, . . . may be replete with happiness and glory. . . . What now becomes of the consideration of our Earth and of its denizens? Does it not dwindle to something incomparably less than a physical point, since our Earth is but a point compared with the distance of the fixed stars. Thus the part of the Universe which we know, being almost lost in nothingness compared with that which is unknown to us, but which we are yet obliged to admit; and all the evils that we know lying in this almost-nothing; it follows that the evils may be almost-nothing in comparison with the goods that the Universe contains.

Leibnitz continues elsewhere:

There is a kind of justice which aims neither at the amendment of the criminal, nor at furnishing an example to others, nor at the reparation of the injury. This justice is founded in pure fitness, which finds a certain satisfaction in the expiation of a wicked deed. The Socinians and Hobbes objected to this punitive justice, which is properly vindictive justice, and which God has reserved for himself at many junctures. . . . It is always founded in the fitness of things, and satisfies not only the offended party, but all wise lookers-on, even as beautiful music or a fine piece of architecture satisfies a well-constituted mind. It is thus that the torments of the damned continue, even tho they serve no longer to turn any one away from sin, and that the rewards of the blest continue, even tho they confirm no one in good ways. The damned draw to themselves ever new penalties by their continuing sins, and the blest attract ever fresh joys by their unceasing progress in good. Both facts are founded on the principle of fitness, . . . for God has made all things harmonious in perfection as I have already said.

Leibnitz's feeble grasp of reality is too obvious to need comment from me. It is evident that no realistic image of the experience of a damned soul had ever approached the portals of his mind. Nor had it occurred to him that the smaller is the number of 'samples' of the genus 'lost-soul' whom God throws as a sop to the eternal fitness, the more unequitably grounded is the glory of the blest. What he gives us is a cold literary exercise, whose cheerful substance even hell-fire does not warm.

And do not tell me that to show the shallowness of rationalist philosophizing I have had to go back to a shallow wig-pated age. The optimism of present-day rationalism sounds just as shallow to the fact-loving mind. The actual universe is a thing wide open, but rationalism makes systems, and systems must be closed. For men in practical life perfection is something far off and still in process of achievement. This for rationalism is but the illusion of the finite and relative: the absolute ground of things is a perfection eternally complete.

I find a fine example of revolt against the airy and shallow optimism of current religious philosophy in a publication of that valiant anarchistic writer Morrison I. Swift. Mr. Swift's anarchism goes a little farther than mine does, but I confess that I sympathize a good deal, and some of you, I know, will sympathize heartily with his dissatisfaction with the idealistic optimisms now in vogue. He begins his pamphlet on 'Human Submission' with a series of city reporter's items from newspapers (suicides, deaths from starvation, and the like) as specimens of our civilized régime. For instance:

After trudging through the snow from one end of the city to the other in the vain hope of securing employment, and with his wife and six children without food and ordered to leave their home in an upper east-side tenement-house because of non-payment of rent, John Corcoran, a clerk, to-day ended his life by drinking carbolic acid. Corcoran lost his position three weeks ago through illness, and during the period of idleness his scanty savings disappeared. Yesterday he obtained work with a gang of city snow-shovelers, but he was too weak from illness, and was forced to quit after an hour's trial with the shovel. Then the weary task of looking for employment was again resumed. Thoroughly dicouraged, Corcoran returned to his home last night to find his wife and children without food and the notice of dispossession on the door. On the following morning he drank the poison.

The records of many more such cases lie before me [Mr. Swift goes on]; an encyclopedia might easily be filled with their kind. These few I cite as an interpretation of the Universe. "We are aware of the presence of God in his world," says a writer in a recent English review. [The very presence of ill in the temporal order is the condition of the perfection of the eternal order, writes Professor Royce (The World and the Individual, II, 385).] "The Absolute is the richer for every discord and for all the diversity which it embraces," says F. H. Bradley (Appearance and Reality, 204). He means that these slain men make the universe richer, and that is philosophy. But while Professors Royce and Bradley and a whole host of guileless thoroughfed thinkers are unveiling Reality and the Absolute and explaining away evil and pain, this is the condition of the only beings known to us anywhere in the universe with a developed consciousness of what the universe is. What these people experience *is* Reality. It gives us an absolute phase of the universe. It is the personal experience of those best qualified in our circle of knowledge to *have* experience, to tell us *what is*. Now what does *thinking about* the experience of these persons come to, compared to directly and personally feeling it as they feel it? The philosophers are dealing in shades, while those who live and feel know truth. And the mind of mankind — not yet the mind of philosophers and of the proprietary class — but of the great mass of the silently thinking men and feeling men, is coming to this view. They are judging the universe as they have hitherto permitted the hierophants of religion and learning to judge *them*. . . .

This Cleveland workingman, killing his children and himself [another of the cited cases] is one of the elemental stupendous facts of this modern world and of this universe. It cannot be glozed over or minimized away by all the treatises on God, and Love, and Being, helplessly existing in their monumental vacuity. This is one of the simple irreducible elements of this world's life, after millions of years of opportunity and twenty centuries of Christ. It is in the mental world what atoms or sub-atoms are in the physical, primary, indestructible. And what it blazons to man is the imposture of all philosophy which does not see in such events the consummate factor of all conscious experience. These facts invincibly prove religion a nullity. Man will not give religion two thousand

centuries or twenty centuries more to try itself and waste human time. Its time is up; its probation is ended; its own record ends it. Mankind has not æons and eternities to spare for trying out discredited systems.[1]

Such is the reaction of an empiricist mind upon the rationalist bill of fare. It is an absolute 'No, I thank you.' "Religion," says Mr. Swift, "is like a sleep-walker to whom actual things are blank." And such, tho possibly less tensely charged with feeling, is the verdict of every seriously inquiring amateur in philosophy to-day who turns to the philosophy-professors for the wherewithal to satisfy the fullness of his nature's needs. Empiricist writers give him a materialism, rationalists give him something religious, but to that religion 'actual things are blank.' He becomes thus the judge of us philosophers. Tender or tough, he finds us wanting. None of us may treat his verdicts disdainfully, for after all, his is the typically perfect mind, the mind the sum of whose demands is greatest, the mind whose criticisms and dissatisfactions are fatal in the long run.

It is at this point that my own solution begins to appear. I offer the oddly-named thing pragmatism as a philosophy that can satisfy both kinds of demand. It can remain religious like the rationalisms, but at the same time, like the empiricisms, it can preserve the richest intimacy with facts. I hope I may be able to leave many of you with as favorable an opinion of it as I preserve myself. Yet, as I am near the end of my hour, I will not introduce pragmatism bodily now. I will begin with it on the stroke of the clock next time. I prefer at the present moment to return a little on what I have said.

[1] Morrison I. Swift, *Human Submission*, Part Second, Philadelphia, Liberty Press, 1905, pp. 4–10.

If any of you here are professional philosophers, and some of you I know to be such, you will doubtless have felt my discourse so far to have been crude in an unpardonable, nay, in an almost incredible degree. Tender-minded and tough-minded, what a barbaric disjunction! And, in general, when philosophy is all compacted of delicate intellectualities and subtleties and scrupulosities, and when every possible sort of combination and transition obtains within its bounds, what a brutal caricature and reduction of highest things to the lowest possible expression is it to represent its field of conflict as a sort of rough-and-tumble fight between two hostile temperaments! What a childishly external view! And again, how stupid it is to treat the abstractness of rationalist systems as a crime, and to damn them because they offer themselves as sanctuaries and places of escape, rather than as prolongations of the world of facts. Are not all our theories just remedies and places of escape? And, if philosophy is to be religious, how can she be anything else than a place of escape from the crassness of reality's surface? What better thing can she do than raise us out of our animal senses and show us another and a nobler home for our minds in that great framework of ideal principles subtending all reality, which the intellect divines? How can principles and general views ever be anything but abstract outlines? Was Cologne cathedral built without an architect's plan on paper? Is refinement in itself an abomination? Is concrete rudeness the only thing that's true?

Believe me, I feel the full force of the indictment. The picture I have given is indeed monstrously over-simplified and rude. But like all abstractions, it will prove to have its use. If philosophers can treat the life of the universe abstractly, they must not complain of an abstract treatment of the life of philosophy itself. In point of fact the picture I have given is, however coarse and sketchy, literally true. Temperaments with their cravings and refusals do determine men in their philosophies, and always will. The details of systems may be reasoned out piecemeal, and when the student is working at a system, he may often forget the forest for the single tree. But when the labor is accomplished, the mind always performs its big summarizing act, and the system forthwith stands over against one like a living thing, with that strange simple note of individuality which haunts our memory, like the wraith of the man, when a friend or enemy of ours is dead.

Not only Walt Whitman could write 'who touches this book touches a man.' The books of all the great philosophers are like so many men. Our sense of an essential personal flavor in each one of them, typical but indescribable, is the finest fruit of our own accomplished philosophic education. What the system pretends to be is a picture of the great universe of God. What it is, — and oh so flagrantly! — is the revelation of how intensely odd the personal flavor of some fellow creature is. Once reduced to these terms (and all our philosophies get reduced to them in minds made critical by learning) our commerce with the systems reverts to the informal, to the instinctive human reaction of satisfaction or dislike. We grow as peremptory in our rejection or admission, as when a person presents himself as a candidate for our favor; our verdicts are couched in as simple adjectives of praise or dispraise. We measure the total character of the universe as we feel it, against the flavor of the philosophy proffered us, and one word is enough.

'Statt der lebendigen Natur,' we say, 'da Gott die Menschen schuf hinein,'— that nebulous concoction, that wooden, that straightlaced thing, that crabbed artificiality, that musty schoolroom product, that sick man's dream! Away with it. Away with all of them! Impossible! Impossible!

Our work over the details of his system is indeed what gives us our resultant impression of the philosopher, but it is on the resultant impression itself that we react. Expertness in philosophy is measured by the definiteness of our summarizing reactions, by the immediate perceptive epithet with which the expert hits such complex objects off. But great expertness is not necessary for the epithet to come. Few people have definitely articulated philosophies of their own. But almost every one has his own peculiar sense of a certain total character in the universe, and of the inadequacy fully to match it of the peculiar systems that he knows. They don't just cover *his* world. One will be too dapper, another too pedantic, a third too much of a joblot of opinions, a fourth too morbid, and a fifth too artificial, or what not. At any rate he and we know off-hand that such philosophies are out of plumb and out of key and out of 'whack,' and have no business to speak up in the universe's name. Plato, Locke, Spinoza, Mill, Caird, Hegel — I prudently avoid names nearer home! — I am sure that to many of you, my hearers, these names are little more than reminders of as many curious personal ways of falling short. It would be an obvious absurdity if such ways of taking the universe were actually true.

We philosophers have to reckon with such feelings on your part. In the last resort, I repeat, it will be by them that all our philosophies shall ultimately be judged. The finally victorious way of looking at things will be the most completely *impressive* way to the normal run of minds.

One word more — namely about philosophies necessarily being abstract outlines. There are outlines and outlines, outlines of buildings that are *fat*, conceived in the cube by their planner, and outlines of buildings invented flat on paper, with the aid of ruler and compass. These remain skinny and emaciated even when set up in stone and mortar, and the outline already suggests that result. An outline in itself is meagre, truly, but it does not necessarily suggest a meagre thing. It is the essential meagreness of *what is suggested* by the usual rationalistic philosophies that moves empiricists to their gesture of rejection. The case of Herbert Spencer's system is much to the point here. Rationalists feel his fearful array of insufficiencies. His dry schoolmaster temperament, the hurdy-gurdy monotony of him, his preference for cheap makeshifts in argument, his lack of education even in mechanical principles, and in general the vagueness of all his fundamental ideas, his whole system wooden, as if knocked together out of cracked hemlock boards — and yet the half of England wants to bury him in Westminster Abbey.

Why? Why does Spencer call out so much reverence in spite of his weakness in rationalistic eyes? Why should so many educated men who feel that weakness, you and I perhaps, wish to see him in the Abbey notwithstanding?

Simply because we feel his heart to be *in the right place* philosophically. His principles may be all skin and bone, but at any rate his books try to mould themselves upon the particular shape of this particular world's carcase. The noise of facts resounds through all his chapters, the citations of fact never cease, he emphasizes facts, turns his face towards their quarter; and that is enough. It means the right *kind* of thing for the empiricist mind.

The pragmatistic philosophy of which I hope to begin talking in my next lecture preserves as cordial a relation with facts, and, unlike Spencer's philosophy, it neither begins nor ends by turning positive religious constructions out of doors — it treats them cordially as well.

I hope I may lead you to find it just the meditating way of thinking that you require.

What Pragmatism Means

Some years ago, being with a camping party in the mountains, I returned from a solitary ramble to find every one engaged in a ferocious metaphysical dispute. The *corpus* of the dispute was a squirrel — a live squirrel supposed to be clinging to one side of a tree-trunk; while over against the tree's opposite side a human being was imagined to stand. This human witness tries to get sight of the squirrel by moving rapidly round the tree, but no matter how fast he goes, the squirrel moves as fast in the opposite direction, and always keeps the tree between himself and the man, so that never a glimpse of him is caught. The resultant metaphysical problem now is this: *Does the man go round the squirrel or not?* He goes round the tree, sure enough, and the squirrel is on the tree; but does he go round the squirrel? In the unlimited leisure of the wilderness, discussion had been worn threadbare. Every one had taken sides, and was obstinate; and the numbers on both sides were even. Each side, when I appeared therefore appealed to me to make it a majority. Mindful of the scholastic adage that whenever you meet a contradiction you must make a distinction, I immediately sought and

found one, as follows: "Which party is right," I said, "depends on what you *practically mean* by 'going round' the squirrel. If you mean passing from the north of him to the east, then to the south, then to the west, and then to the north of him again, obviously the man does go round him, for he occupies these successive positions. But if on the contrary you mean being first in front of him, then on the right of him, then behind him, then on his left, and finally in front again, it is quite as obvious that the man fails to go round him, for by the compensating movements the squirrel makes, he keeps his belly turned towards the man all the time, and his back turned away. Make the distinction, and there is no occasion for any farther dispute. You are both right and both wrong according as you conceive the verb 'to go round' in one practical fashion or the other."

Although one or two of the hotter disputants called my speech a shuffling evasion, saying they wanted no quibbling or scholastic hairsplitting, but meant just plain honest English 'round,' the majority seemed to think that the distinction had assuaged the dispute.

I tell this trivial anecdote because it is a peculiarly simple example of what I wish now to speak of as *the pragmatic method*. The pragmatic method is primarily a method of settling metaphysical disputes that otherwise might be interminable. Is the world one or many? — fated or free? — material or spiritual? — here are notions either of which may or may not hold good of the world; and disputes over such notions are unending. The pragmatic method in such cases is to try to interpret each notion by tracing its respective practical consequences. What difference would it practically make to any one if this notion rather than that notion were true? If no practical difference whatever can be traced, then the alternatives mean practically the same thing, and all dispute is idle. Whenever a dispute is serious, we ought to be able to show some practical difference that must follow from one side or the other's being right.

A glance at the history of the idea will show you still better what pragmatism means. The term is derived from the same Greek word πράγμα, meaning action, from which our words 'practice' and 'practical' come. It was first introduced into philosophy by Mr. Charles Peirce in 1878. In an article entitled 'How to Make Our Ideas Clear,' in the 'Popular Science Monthly' for January of that year[2] Mr. Peirce, after pointing out that our beliefs are really rules for action, said that, to develop a thought's meaning, we need only determine what conduct it is fitted to produce: that conduct is for us its sole significance. And the tangible fact at the root of all our thought-distinctions, however subtle, is that there is no one of them so fine as to consist in anything but a possible difference of practice. To attain perfect clearness in our thoughts of an object, then, we need only consider what conceivable effects of a practical kind the object may involve — what sensations we are to expect from it, and what reactions we must prepare. Our conception of these effects, whether immediate or remote, is then for us the whole of our conception of the object, so far as that conception has positive significance at all.

This is the principle of Peirce, the principle of pragmatism. It lay entirely unnoticed by any one for twenty years, until I, in an address before Professor Howison's philosophical union at the university of California, brought it forward

2 Translated in the *Revue Philosophique* for January, 1879 (vol. vii).

again and made a special application of it to religion. By that date (1898) the times seemed ripe for its reception. The word 'pragmatism' spread, and at present it fairly spots the pages of the philosophic journals. On all hands we find the 'pragmatic movement' spoken of, sometimes with respect, sometimes with contumely, seldom with clear understanding. It is evident that the term applies itself conveniently to a number of tendencies that hitherto have lacked a collective name, and that it has 'come to stay.'

To take in the importance of Peirce's principle, one must get accustomed to applying it to concrete cases. I found a few years ago that Ostwald, the illustrious Leipzig chemist, had been making perfectly distinct use of the principle of pragmatism in his lectures on the philosophy of science, though he had not called it by that name.

"All realities influence our practice," he wrote me, "and that influence is their meaning for us. I am accustomed to put questions to my classes in this way: In what respects would the world be different if this alternative or that were true? If I can find nothing that would become different, then the alternative has no sense."

That is, the rival views mean practically the same thing, and meaning, other than practical, there is for us none. Ostwald in a published lecture gives this example of what he means. Chemists have long wrangled over the inner constitution of certain bodies called 'tautomerous.' Their properties seemed equally consistent with the notion that an instable hydrogen atom oscillates inside of them, or that they are instable mixtures of two bodies. Controversy raged, but never was decided. "It would never have begun," says Ostwald, "if the combatants had asked themselves what particular experimental fact could have been made different by one or the other view being correct. For it would then have appeared that no difference of fact could possibly ensue; and the quarrel was as unreal as if, theorizing in primitive times about the raising of dough by yeast, one party should have invoked a 'brownie,' while another insisted on an 'elf' as the true cause of the phenomenon."[3]

It is astonishing to see how many philosophical disputes collapse into insignificance the moment you subject them to this simple test of tracing a concrete consequence. There can *be* no difference anywhere that does n't *make* a difference elsewhere — no difference in abstract truth that does n't express itself in a difference in concrete fact and in conduct consequent upon that fact, imposed on somebody, somehow, somewhere, and somewhen. The whole function of philosophy ought to be to find out what definite difference it will make to you and me, at definite instants of our life, if this world-formula or that world-formula be the true one.

There is absolutely nothing new in the pragmatic method. Socrates was an adept at it. Aristotle used it methodically. Locke, Berkeley, and Hume made momentous contributions to truth by its means. Shadworth Hodgson keeps insisting that realities are only what they are 'known as.' But these forerunners of pragmatism used it in fragments: they were preluders only. Not until in our

[3] 'Theorie und Praxis,' *Zeitsch. des Oesterreichischen Ingenieur u. Architecten-Vereines*, 1905, Nr. 4 u. 6. I find a still more radical pragmatism than Ostwald's in an address by Professor W. S. Franklin: "I think that the sickliest notion of physics, even if a student gets it, is that it is 'the science of masses, molecules, and the ether.' And I think that the healthiest notion, even if a student does not wholly get it, is that physics is the science of the ways of taking hold of bodies and pushing them!" (*Science*, January 2, 1903.)

time has it generalized itself, become conscious of a universal mission, pretended to a conquering destiny. I believe in that destiny, and I hope I may end by inspiring you with my belief.

Pragmatism represents a perfectly familiar attitude in philosophy, the empiricist attitude, but it represents it, as it seems to me, both in a more radical and in a less objectionable form than it has ever yet assumed. A pragmatist turns his back resolutely and once for all upon a lot of inveterate habits dear to professional philosophers. He turns away from abstraction and insufficiency, from verbal solution, from bad *a priori* reasons, from fixed principles, closed systems, and pretended absolutes and origins. He turns towards concreteness and adequacy, towards facts, towards action and towards power. That means the empiricist temper regnant and the rationalist temper sincerely given up. It means the open air and possibilities of nature, as against dogma, artificiality, and the pretence of finality in truth.

At the same time it does not stand for any special results. It is a method only. But the general triumph of that method would mean an enormous change in what I called in my last lecture the 'temperament' of philosophy. Teachers of the ultra-rationalistic type would be frozen out, much as the courtier type is frozen out in republics, as the ultramontane type of priest is frozen out in protestant lands. Science and metaphysics would come much nearer together, would in fact work absolutely hand in hand.

Metaphysics has usually followed a very primitive kind of quest. You know how men have always hankered after unlawful magic, and you know what a great part in magic *words* have always played. If you have his name, or the formula of incantation that binds him, you can control the spirit, genie, afrite, or whatever the power may be. Solomon knew the names of all the spirits, and having their names, he held them subject to his will. So the universe has always appeared to the natural mind as a kind of enigma, of which the key must be sought in the shape of some illuminating or power-bringing word or name. That word names the universe's *principle,* and to possess it is after a fashion to possess the universe itself. 'God,' 'Matter,' 'Reason,' 'the Absolute,' 'Energy,' are so many solving names. You can rest when you have them. You are at the end of your metaphysical quest.

But if you follow the pragmatic method, you cannot look on any such word as closing your quest. You must bring out of each word its practical cash-value, set it at work within the stream of your experience. It appears less as a solution, then, than as a program for more work, and more particularly as an indication of the ways in which existing realities may be *changed.*

Theories thus become instruments, not answers to enigmas, in which we can rest. We don't lie back upon them, we move forward, and, on occasion, make nature over again by their aid. Pragmatism unstiffens all our theories, limbers them up and sets each one at work. Being nothing essentially new, it harmonizes with many ancient philosophic tendencies. It agrees with nominalism for instance, in always appealing to particulars; with utilitarianism in emphasizing practical aspects; with positivism in its disdain for verbal solutions, useless questions and metaphysical abstractions.

All these, you see, are *anti-intellectualist* tendencies. Against rationalism as a pretension and a method pragmatism is fully armed and militant. But, at the outset, at least, it stands for no particular results. It has no dogmas, and no doctrines save its method. As the young Italian pragmatist Papini has well said, it lies in the midst of our theories, like a corridor in a hotel. Innumerable chambers open out of it. In one you may find a man writing an atheistic volume; in the next some one on his knees praying for faith and strength; in a third a chemist investigating a body's properties. In a fourth a system of idealistic metaphysics is being excogitated; in a fifth the impossibility of metaphysics is being shown. But they all own the corridor, and all must pass through it if they want a practicable way of getting into or out of their respective rooms.

No particular results then, so far, but only an attitude of orientation, is what the pragmatic method means. *The attitude of looking away from first things, principles, 'categories,' supposed necessities; and of looking towards last things, fruits, consequences, facts.*

So much for the pragmatic method! You may say that I have been praising it rather than explaining it to you, but I shall presently explain it abundantly enough by showing how it works on some familiar problems. Meanwhile the word pragmatism has come to be used in a still wider sense, as meaning also a certain *theory of truth.* I mean to give a whole lecture to the statement of that theory, after first paving the way, so I can be very brief now. But brevity is hard to follow, so I ask for your redoubled attention for a quarter of an hour. If much remains obscure, I hope to make it clearer in the later lectures.

One of the most successfully cultivated branches of philosophy in our time is what is called inductive logic, the study of the conditions under which our sciences have evolved. Writers on this subject have begun to show a singular unanimity as to what the laws of nature and elements of fact mean, when formulated by mathematicians, physicists and chemists. When the first mathematical, logical, and natural uniformities, the first *laws*, were discovered, men were so carried away by the clearness, beauty and simplification that resulted, that they believed themselves to have deciphered authentically the eternal thoughts of the Almighty. His mind also thundered and reverberated in syllogisms. He also thought in conic sections, squares and roots and ratios, and geometrized like Euclid. He made Kepler's laws for the planets to follow; he made velocity increase proportionally to the time in falling bodies; he made the law of the sines for light to obey when refracted; he established the classes, orders, families and genera of plants and animals, and fixed the distances between them. He thought the archetypes of all things, and devised their variations; and when we rediscover any one of these his wondrous institutions, we seize his mind in its very literal intention.

But as the sciences have developed farther, the notion has gained ground that most, perhaps all, of our laws are only approximations. The laws themselves, moreover, have grown so numerous that there is no counting them; and so many rival formulations are proposed in all the branches of science that investigators have become accustomed to the notion that no theory is absolutely a transcript of reality, but that any one of them may from some point of view be useful. Their great use is to summarize old facts and to lead to new ones. They are only a man-made language, a conceptual shorthand, as some one calls them, in which we write our reports of nature; and languages, as is well known, tolerate much choice of expression and many dialects.

Thus human arbitrariness has driven divine necessity from scientific logic. If I mention the names of Sigwart, Mach, Ostwald, Pearson, Milhaud, Poincaré, Duhem, Ruyssen, those of you who are students will easily identify the tendency I speak of, and will think of additional names.

Riding now on the front of this wave of scientific logic Messrs. Schiller and Dewey appear with their pragmatistic account of what truth everywhere signifies. Everywhere, these teachers say, 'truth' in our ideas and beliefs means the same thing that it means in science. It means, they say, nothing but this, *that ideas (which themselves are but parts of our experience) become true just in so far as they help us to get into satisfactory relation with other parts of our experience*, to summarize them and get about among them by conceptual short-cuts instead of following the interminable succession of particular phenomena. Any idea upon which we can ride, so to speak; any idea that will carry us prosperously from any one part of our experience to any other part, linking things satisfactorily, working securely, simplifying, saving labor; is true for just so much, true in so far forth, true *instrumentally*. This is the 'instrumental' view of truth taught so successfully at Chicago, the view that truth in our ideas means their power to 'work,' promulgated so brilliantly at Oxford.

Messrs. Dewey, Schiller and their allies, in reaching this general conception of all truth, have only followed the example of geologists, biologists and philologists. In the establishment of these other sciences, the successful stroke was always to take some simple process actually observable in operation — as denudation by weather, say, or variation from parental type, or change of dialect by incorporation of new words and pronunciations — and then to generalize it, making it apply to all times, and produce great results by summating its effects through the ages.

The observable process which Schiller and Dewey particularly singled out for generalization is the familiar one by which any individual settles into *new opinions*. The process here is always the same. The individual has a stock of old opinions already, but he meets a new experience that puts them to a strain. Somebody contradicts them; or in a reflective moment he discovers that they contradict each other; or he hears of facts with which they are incompatible; or desires arise in him which they cease to satisfy. The result is an inward trouble to which his mind till then had been a stranger, and from which he seeks to escape by modifying his previous mass of opinions. He saves as much of it as he can, for in this matter of belief we are all extreme conservatives. So he tries to change first this opinion, and then that (for they resist change very variously), until at last some new idea comes up which he can graft upon the ancient stock with a minimum of disturbance of the latter, some idea that mediates between the stock and the new experience and runs them into one another most felicitously and expediently.

This new idea is then adopted as the true one. It preserves the older stock of truths with a minimum of modification, stretching them just enough to make them admit the novelty, but conceiving that in ways as familiar as the case leaves possible. An *outrée* explanation, violating all our preconceptions, would never pass for a true account of a novelty. We should scratch round industriously till we found something less eccentric. The most violent revolutions in an individual's beliefs leave most of his old order standing. Time and space, cause and effect, nature and history, and one's own biography remain untouched. New truth is always a go-between, a smoother-over of transitions. It marries old opinion to new fact so as ever to show a minimum of jolt, a maximum of continuity. We hold a theory true just in proportion to its success in solving this 'problem of maxima and minima.' But success in solving this problem is eminently a matter of approximation. We say this theory solves it on the whole more satisfactorily than that theory; but that means more satisfactorily to ourselves, and individuals will emphasize their points of satisfaction differently. To a certain degree, therefore, everything here is plastic.

The point I now urge you to observe particularly is the part played by the older truths. Failure to take account of it is the source of much of the unjust criticism levelled against pragmatism. Their influence is absolutely controlling. Loyalty to them is the first principle — in most cases it is the only principle; for by far the most usual way of handling phenomena so novel that they would make for a serious rearrangement of our preconception is to ignore them altogether, or to abuse those who bear witness for them.

You doubtless wish examples of this process of truth's growth, and the only trouble is their superabundance. The simplest case of new truth is of course the mere numerical addition of new kinds of facts, or of new single facts of old kinds, to our experience — an addition that involves no alteration in the old beliefs. Day follows day, and its contents are simply added. The new contents themselves are not true, they simply *come* and *are*. Truth is *what we say about* them, and when we say that they have come, truth is satisfied by the plain additive formula.

But often the day's contents oblige a rearrangement. If I should now utter piercing shrieks and act like a maniac on this platform, it would make many of you revise your ideas as to the probable worth of my philosophy. 'Radium' came the other day as part of the day's content, and seemed for a moment to contradict our ideas of the whole order of nature, that order having come to be identified with what is called the conservation of energy. The mere sight of radium paying heat away indefinitely out of its own pocket seemed to violate that conservation. What to think? If the radiations from it were nothing but an escape of unsuspected 'potential' energy, preexistent inside of the atoms, the principle of conservation would be saved. The discovery of 'helium' as the radiation's outcome, opened a way to this belief. So Ramsay's view is generally held to be true, because, although it extends our old ideas of energy, it causes a minimum of alteration in their nature.

I need not multiply instances. A new opinion counts as 'true' just in proportion as it gratifies the individual's desire to assimilate the novel in his experience to his beliefs in stock. It must both lean on old truth and grasp new fact; and its success (as I said a moment ago) in doing this, is a matter for the individual's appreciation. When old truth grows, then, by new truth's addition, it is for subjective reasons. We are in the process and obey the reasons. That new idea is truest which performs most felicitously its function of satisfying our double urgency. It makes itself true, gets itself classed as true, by the way it works; grafting itself then upon the ancient body of truth, which thus grows much as a tree grows by the activity of a new layer of cambium.

Now Dewey and Schiller proceed to generalize this observation and to apply it to the most ancient parts of truth. They also once were plastic. They also were called true for human reasons. They also mediated between still earlier truths and what in those days were novel observations. Purely objective truth, truth in whose establishment the function of giving human satisfaction in marrying previous parts of experience with newer parts played no rôle whatever, is nowhere to be found. The reasons why we call things true is the reason why they *are* true, for 'to be true' *means* only to perform this marriage-function.

The trail of the human serpent is thus over everything. Truth independent; truth that we *find* merely; truth no longer malleable to human need; truth incorrigible, in a word; such truth exists indeed superabundantly — or is supposed to exist by rationalistically minded thinkers; but then it means only the dead heart of the living tree, and its being there means only that truth also has its paleontology, and its 'prescription,' and may grow stiff with years of veteran service and petrified in men's regard by sheer antiquity. But how plastic even the oldest truths nevertheless really are has been vividly shown in our day by the transformation of logical and mathematical ideas, a transformation which seems even to be invading physics. The ancient formulas are reinterpreted as special expressions of much wider principles, principles that our ancestors never got a glimpse of in their present shape and formulation.

Mr. Schiller still gives to all this view of truth the name of 'Humanism,' but, for this doctrine too, the name of pragmatism seems fairly to be in the ascendant, so I will treat it under the name of pragmatism in these lectures.

Such then would be the scope of pragmatism — first, a method; and second, a genetic theory of what is meant by truth. And these two things must be our future topics.

What I have said of the theory of truth will, I am sure, have appeared obscure and unsatisfactory to most of you by reason of its brevity. I shall make amends for that hereafter. In a lecture on 'common sense' I shall try to show what I mean by truths grown petrified by antiquity. In another lecture I shall expatiate on the idea that our thoughts become true in proportion as they successfully exert their go-between function. In a third I shall show how hard it is to discriminate subjective from objective factors in Truth's development. You may not follow me wholly in these lectures; and if you do, you may not wholly agree with me. But you will, I know, regard me at least as serious, and treat my effort with respectful consideration.

You will probably be surprised to learn, then, that Messrs. Schiller's and Dewey's theories have suffered a hailstorm of contempt and ridicule. All rationalism has risen against them. In influential quarters Mr. Schiller, in particular, has been treated like an impudent schoolboy who deserves a spanking. I should not mention this, but for the fact that it throws so much sidelight upon that rationalistic temper to which I have opposed the temper of pragmatism. Pragmatism is uncomfortable away from facts. Rationalism is comfortable only in the presence of abstractions. This pragmatist talk about truths in the plural, about their utility and satisfactoriness, about the success with which they 'work,' etc., suggests to the typical intellectualist mind a sort of coarse lame second-rate makeshift article of truth. Such truths are not real truth. Such tests are merely subjective. As against this, objective truth must be something non-utilitarian, haughty, refined, remote, august, exalted.

It must be an absolute correspondence of our thoughts with an equally absolute reality. It must be what we *ought* to think unconditionally. The conditioned ways in which we *do* think are so much irrelevance and matter for psychology. Down with psychology, up with logic, in all this question!

See the exquisite contrast of the types of mind! The pragmatist clings to facts and concreteness, observes truth at its work in particular cases, and generalizes. Truth, for him, becomes a class-name for all sorts of definite working-values in experience. For the rationalist it remains a pure abstraction, to the bare name of which we must defer. When the pragmatist undertakes to show in detail just *why* we must defer, the rationalist is unable to recognize the concretes from which his own abstraction is taken. He accuses us of *denying* truth; whereas we have only sought to trace exactly why people follow it and always ought to follow it. Your typical ultra-abstractionist fairly shudders at concreteness: other things equal, he positively prefers the pale and spectral. If the two universes were offered, he would always choose the skinny outline rather than the rich thicket of reality. It is so much purer, clearer, nobler.

I hope that as these lectures go on, the concreteness and closeness to facts of the pragmatism which they advocate may be what approves itself to you as its most satisfactory peculiarity. It only follows here the example of the sister-sciences, interpreting the unobserved by the observed. It brings old and new harmoniously together. It converts the absolutely empty notion of a static relation of 'correspondence' (what that may mean we must ask later) between our minds and reality, into that of a rich and active commerce (that any one may follow in detail and understand) between particular thoughts of ours, and the great universe of other experiences in which they play their parts and have their uses.

But enough of this at present? The justification of what I say must be postponed. I wish now to add a word in further explanation of the claim I made at our last meeting, that pragmatism may be a happy harmonizer of empiricist ways of thinking with the more religious demands of human beings.

Men who are strongly of the fact-loving temperament, you may remember me to have said, are liable to be kept at a distance by the small sympathy with facts which that philosophy from the present-day fashion of idealism offers them. It is far too intellectualistic. Old fashioned theism was bad enough, with its notion of God as an exalted monarch, made up of a lot of unintelligible or preposterous 'attributes'; but, so long as it held strongly by the argument from design, it kept some touch with concrete realities. Since, however, darwinism has once for all displaced design from the minds of the 'scientific,' theism has lost that foothold; and some kind of an immanent or pantheistic deity working *in* things rather than above them is, if any, the kind recommended to our contemporary imagination. Aspirants to a philosophic religion turn, as a rule, more hopefully nowadays towards idealistic pantheism than towards the older dualistic theism, in spite of the fact that the latter still counts able defenders.

But, as I said in my first lecture, the brand of pantheism offered is hard for them to assimilate if they are lovers of facts, or empirically minded. It is the absolutistic brand, spurning the dust and reared upon pure logic. It keeps no connexion whatever with concreteness. Affirming the Absolute Mind, which is its substitute for God, to be the rational pre-supposition of all particulars of fact, whatever they may be, it remains supremely indifferent to what the particular facts in our world actually are. Be they what they may, the Absolute will father them. Like the sick lion in Esop's fable, all footprints lead into his den, but *nulla vestigia retrorsum.* You cannot redescend into the world of particulars by the Absolute's aid, or deduce any necessary consequences of detail important for your life from your idea of his nature. He gives you indeed the assurance that all is well with *Him,* and for his eternal way of thinking; but thereupon he leaves you to be finitely saved by your own temporal devices.

Far be it from me to deny the majesty of this conception, or its capacity to yield religious comfort to a most respectable class of minds. But from the human point of view, no one can pretend that it does n't suffer from the faults of remoteness and abstractness. It is eminently a product of what I have ventured to call the rationalistic temper. It disdains empiricism's needs. It substitutes a pallid outline for the real world's richness. It is dapper, it is noble in the bad sense, in the sense in which to be noble is to be inapt for humble service. In this real world of sweat and dirt, it seems to me that when a view of things is 'noble,' that ought to count as a presumption against its truth, and as a philosophic disqualification. The prince of darkness may be a gentleman, as we are told he is, but whatever the God of earth and heaven is, he can surely be no gentleman. His menial services are needed in the dust of our human trials, even more than his dignity is needed in the empyrean.

Now pragmatism, devoted though she be to facts, has no such materialistic bias as ordinary empiricism labors under. Moreover, she has no objection whatever to the realizing of abstractions, so long as you get about among particulars with their aid and they actually carry you somewhere. Interested in no conclusions but those which our minds and our experiences work out together, she has no *a priori* prejudices against theology. *If theological ideas prove to have a value for concrete life, they will be true, for pragmatism, in the sense of being good for so much. For how much more they are true, will depend entirely on their relations to the other truths that also have to be acknowledged.*

What I said just now about the Absolute, of transcendental idealism, is a case in point. First, I called it majestic and said it yielded religious comfort to a class of minds, and then I accused it of remoteness and sterility. But so far as it affords such comfort, it surely is not sterile; it has that amount of value; it performs a concrete function. As a good pragmatist, I myself ought to call the Absolute true 'in so far forth,' then; and I unhesitatingly now do so.

But what does *true in so far forth* mean in this case? To answer, we need only apply the pragmatic method. What do believers in the Absolute mean by saying that their belief affords them comfort? They mean that since, in the Absolute finite evil is 'overruled' already, we may, therefore, whenever we wish, treat the temporal as if it were potentially the eternal, be sure that we can trust its outcome, and, without sin, dismiss our fear and drop the worry of our finite responsibility. In short, they mean that we have a right ever and anon to take a moral holiday, to let the world wag in its own way, feeling that its issues are in better hands than ours and are none of our business.

The universe is a system of which the individual members may relax their anxieties occasionally, in which the don't-care mood is also right for men, and moral holidays in order, — that, if I mistake not, is part, at least, of what the Absolute is 'known-as,' that is the great difference in our particular experiences which his being true makes, for us, that is his cash-value when he is pragmatically interpreted. Farther than that the ordinary lay-reader in philosophy who thinks favorably of absolute idealism does not venture to sharpen his conceptions. He can use the Absolute for so much, and so much is very precious. He is pained at hearing you speak incredulously of the Absolute, therefore, and disregards your criticisms because they deal with aspects of the conception that he fails to follow.

If the Absolute means this, and means no more than this, who can possibly deny the truth of it? To deny it would be to insist that men should never relax, and that holidays are never in order.

I am well aware how odd it must seem to some of you to hear me say that an idea is 'true' so long as to believe it is profitable to our lives. That it is *good*, for as much as it profits, you will gladly admit. If what we do by its aid is good, you will allow the idea itself to be good in so far forth, for we are the better for possessing it. But is it not a strange misuse of the word 'truth,' you will say, to call ideas also 'true' for this reason?

To answer this difficulty fully is impossible at this stage of my account. You touch here upon the very central point of Messrs. Schiller's, Dewey's and my own doctrine of truth, which I can not discuss with detail until my sixth lecture. Let me now say only this, that truth is *one species of good*, and not, as is usually supposed, a category distinct from good, and co-ordinate with it. *The true is the name of whatever proves itself to be good in the way of belief, and good, too, for definite, assignable reasons.* Surely you must admit this, that if there were *no* good for life in true ideas, or if the knowledge of them were positively disadvantageous and false ideas the only useful ones, then the current notion that truth is divine and precious, and its pursuit a duty, could never have grown up or become a dogma. In a world like that, our duty would be to *shun* truth, rather. But in this world, just as certain foods are not only agreeable to our taste, but good for our teeth, our stomach, and our tissues; so certain ideas are not only agreeable to think about, or agreeable as supporting other ideas that we are fond of, but they are also helpful in life's practical struggles. If there be any life that it is really better we should lead, and if there be any idea which, if believed in, would help us to lead that life, then it would be really *better for us* to believe in that idea, *unless, indeed, belief in it incidentally clashed with other greater vital benefits.*

'What would be better for us to believe'! This sounds very like a definition of truth. It comes very near to saying 'what we *ought* to believe': and in *that* definition none of you would find any oddity. Ought we ever not to believe what it is *better for us* to believe? And can we then keep the notion of what is better for us, and what is true for us, permanently apart?

Pragmatism says no, and I fully agree with her. Probably you also agree, so far as the abstract statement goes, but with a suspicion that if we practically did believe everything that made for good in our own personal lives, we should be found indulging all kinds of fancies about this world's affairs, and all kinds of sentimental superstitions about a world hereafter. Your suspicion here is

undoubtedly well founded, and it is evident that something happens when you pass from the abstract to the concrete that complicates the situation.

I said just now that what is better for us to believe is true *unless the belief incidentally clashes with some other vital benefit.* Now in real life what vital benefits is any particular belief of ours most liable to clash with? What indeed except the vital benefits yielded by *other beliefs* when these prove incompatible with the first ones? In other words, the greatest enemy of any one of our truths may be the rest of our truths. Truths have once for all this desperate instinct of self-preservation and of desire to extinguish whatever contradicts them. My belief in the Absolute, based on the good it does me, must run the gauntlet of all my other beliefs. Grant that it may be true in giving me a moral holiday. Nevertheless, as I conceive it, — and let me speak now confidentially, as it were, and merely in my own private person, — it clashes with other truths of mine whose benefits I hate to give up on its account. It happens to be associated with a kind of logic of which I am the enemy, I find that it entangles me in metaphysical paradoxes that are inacceptable, etc., etc. But as I have enough trouble in life already without adding the trouble of carrying these intellectual inconsistencies, I personally just give up the Absolute. I just *take* my moral holidays; or else as a professional philosopher, I try to justify them by some other principle.

If I could restrict my notion of the Absolute to its bare holiday-giving value, it would n't clash with my other truths. But we can not easily thus restrict our hypotheses. They carry supernumerary features, and these it is that clash so. My disbelief in the Absolute means then disbelief in those other supernumerary features, for I fully believe in the legitimacy of taking moral holidays.

You see by this what I meant when I called pragmatism a mediator and reconciler and said, borrowing the word from Papini, that she 'unstiffens' our theories. She has in fact no prejudices whatever, no obstructive dogmas, no rigid canons of what shall count as proof. She is completely genial. She will entertain any hypothesis, she will consider any evidence. It follows that in the religious field she is at a great advantage both over positivistic empiricism, with its anti-theological bias, and over religious rationalism, with its exclusive interest in the remote, the noble, the simple, and the abstract in the way of conception.

In short, she widens the field of search for God. Rationalism sticks to logic and the empyrean. Empiricism sticks to the external senses. Pragmatism is willing to take anything, to follow either logic or the senses and to count the humblest and most personal experiences. She will count mystical experiences if they have practical consequences. She will take a God who lives in the very dirt of private fact — if that should seem a likely place to find him.

Her only test of probable truth is what works best in the way of leading us, what fits every part of life best and combines with the collectivity of experience's demands, nothing being omitted. If theological ideas should do this, if the notion of God, in particular, should prove to do it, how could pragmatism possibly deny God's existence? She could see no meaning in treating as 'not true' a notion that was pragmatically so successful. What other kind of truth could there be, for her, than all this agreement with concrete reality?

In my last lecture I shall return again to the relations of pragmatism with religion. But you see already how democratic she is. Her manners are as various and flexible, her resources as rich and endless, and her conclusions as friendly as those of mother nature.

John Dewey: WHAT I BELIEVE

I

FAITH was once almost universally thought to be acceptance of a definite body of intellectual propositions, acceptance being based upon authority — preferably that of revelation from on high. It meant adherence to a creed consisting of set articles. Such creeds are recited daily in our churches. Of late there has developed another conception of faith. This is suggested by the words of an American thinker: "Faith is tendency toward action." According to such a view, faith is the matrix of formulated creeds and the inspiration of endeavor. Change from the one conception of faith to the other is indicative of a profound alteration. Adherence to any body of doctrines and dogmas based upon a specific authority signifies distrust in the power of experience to provide, in its own ongoing movement, the needed principles of be-

Reprinted by permission from *Forum*, LXXXIII, No. 3 (March, 1930), 176–182.

lief and action. Faith in its newer sense signifies that experience itself is the sole ultimate authority.

Such a faith has in it all the elements of a philosophy. For it implies that the course and material of experience give support and stay to life, and that its possibilities provide all the ends and ideals that are to regulate conduct. When these implications are made explicit, there emerges a definite philosophy. I have no intention here of trying to unfold such a philosophy, but rather to indicate what a philosophy based on experience as the ultimate authority in knowledge and conduct means in the present state of civilization, what its reactions are upon what is thought and done. For such a faith is not at present either articulate or widely held. If it were, it would be not so much a philosophy as a part of common sense.

In fact, it goes contrary to the whole trend of the traditions by which mankind is educated. On the whole it has been denied that experience and life can regulate themselves and provide their own means of direction and inspiration. Except for an occasional protest, historic philosophies have been "transcendental." And this trait of philosophies is a reflex of the fact that dominant moral codes and religious beliefs have appealed for support to something above and beyond experience. Experience has been systematically disparaged in contrast with something taken to be more fundamental and superior in worth.

Life as it is actually lived has been treated as a preparation for something outside of it and after it. It has been thought lawless, without meaning and value, except as it was taken to testify to a reality beyond itself. The creeds that have prevailed have been founded upon the supposed necessity of escape from the confusion and uncertainties of experience. Life has been thought to be evil and hopeless unless it could be shown to bear within itself the assured promise of a higher reality. Philosophies of escape have also been philosophies of compensation for the ills and sufferings of the experienced world.

Mankind has hardly inquired what would happen if the possibilities of experience were seriously explored and exploited. There has been much systematic exploration in science and much frantic exploitation in politics, business, and amusement. But this attention has been, so to say, incidental and in contravention to the professedly ruling scheme of belief. It has not been the product of belief in the power of experience to furnish organizing principles and directive ends. Religions have been saturated with the supernatural — and the supernatural signifies precisely that which lies beyond experience. Moral codes have been allied to this religious supernaturalism and have sought their foundation and sanction in it. Contrast with such ideas, deeply embedded in all Western culture, gives the philosophy of faith in experience a definite and profound meaning.

II

Why have men in the past resorted to philosophies of that which is above and beyond experience? And why should it be now thought possible to desist from such recourse? The answer to the first question is, undoubtedly, that the experience which men had, as well as any which they could reasonably anticipate, gave no signs of ability to furnish the means of its own regulation. It offered promises it refused to fulfill; it awakened desires only to frustrate them; it created hopes and blasted them; it evoked ideals and was indifferent and hostile to their realization. Men who were incompetent to cope with the troubles and evils that experience brought with it, naturally distrusted the capacity of experience to give authoritative guidance. Since experience did not contain the arts by which its own course could be directed, philosophies and religions of escape and consolatory compensation naturally ensued.

What are the grounds for supposing that this state of affairs has changed and that it is now possible to put trust in the possibilities of experience itself? The answer to this question supplies the content of a philosophy of experience. There are traits of present experience which were unknown and unpossessed when the ruling beliefs of the past were developed. Experience now owns as a part of itself scientific methods of discovery and test; it is marked by ability to create techniques and technologies — that is, arts which arrange and utilize all sorts of conditions and energies, physical and human. These new possessions give experience and its potentialities a radically new meaning. It is a commonplace that since the seventeenth century science has revolutionized our beliefs about outer nature, and it is also beginning to revolutionize those about man.

When our minds dwell on this extraordinary change, they are likely to think of the transformation that has taken place in the subject matter of astronomy, physics, chemistry, biology, psychology, anthropology, and so on. But great as is this change, it shrinks in comparison with the change that has occurred in method. The latter is the author of the revolution in the content of beliefs. The new methods have, moreover, brought with them a radical change in our intellectual attitude and its attendant morale. The method we term "scientific" forms

for the modern man (and a man is not modern merely because he lives in 1930) the sole dependable means of disclosing the realities of existence. It is the sole authentic mode of revelation. This possession of a new method, to the use of which no limits can be put, signifies a new idea of the nature and possibilities of experience. It imports a new morale of confidence, control, and security.

The change in knowledge has its overt and practical counterpart in what we term the Industrial Revolution, with its creation of arts for directing and using the energies of nature. Technology includes, of course, the engineering arts that have produced the railway, steamship, automobile, and airplane, the telegraph, telephone, and radio, and the printing press. But it also includes new procedures in medicine and hygiene, the function of insurance in all its branches, and, in its potentiality if not actualization, radically new methods in education and other modes of human relationship. "Technology" signifies all the intelligent techniques by which the energies of nature and man are directed and used in satisfaction of human needs; it cannot be limited to a few outer and comparatively mechanical forms. In the face of its possibilities, the traditional conception of experience is obsolete.

Different theories have expressed with more or less success this and that phase of the newer movements. But there is no integration of them into the standing habits and the controlling outlook of men and women. There are two great signs and tests of this fact. In science and in industry the fact of constant change is generally accepted. Moral, religious, and articulate philosophic creeds are based upon the idea of fixity. In the history of the race, change has been feared. It has been looked upon as the source of decay and degeneration. It has been opposed as the cause of disorder, chaos, and anarchy. One chief reason for the appeal to something beyond experience was the fact that experience is always in such flux that men had to seek stability and peace outside of it. Until the seventeenth century, the natural sciences shared in the belief in the superiority of the immutable to the moving, and took for their ideal the discovery of the permanent and changeless. Ruling philosophies, whether materialistic or spiritual, accepted the same notion as their foundation.

In this attachment to the fixed and immutable, both science and philosophy reflected the universal and pervasive conviction of religion and morals. Impermanence meant insecurity; the permanent was the sole ground of assurance and support amid the vicissitudes of existence. Christianity proffered a fixed revelation of absolute, unchanging Being and truth; and the revelation was elaborated into a system of definite rules and ends for the direction of life. Hence "morals" were conceived as a code of laws, the same everywhere and at all times. The good life was one lived in fixed adherence to fixed principles.

III

In contrast with all such beliefs, the outstanding fact in all branches of natural science is that to exist is to be in process, in change. Nevertheless, although the idea of movement and change has made itself at home in the physical sciences, it has had comparatively little influence on the popular mind as the latter looks at religion, morals, economics, and politics. In these fields it is still supposed that our choice is between confusion, anarchy, and something fixed and immutable. It is assumed that Christianity is the final religion; Jesus the com-

plete and unchanging embodiment of the divine and the human. It is assumed that our present economic régime, at least in principle, expresses something final, something to endure — with, it is incidentally hoped, some improvements in detail. It is assumed, in spite of evident flux in the actual situation, that the institutions of marriage and family that developed in medieval Europe are the last and unchanging word.

These examples hint at the extent to which ideals of fixity persist in a moving world. A philosophy of experience will accept at its full value the fact that social and moral existences are, like physical existences, in a state of continuous if obscure change. It will not try to cover up the fact of inevitable modification, and will make no attempt to set fixed limits to the extent of changes that are to occur. For the futile effort to achieve security and anchorage in something fixed, it will substitute the effort to determine the character of changes that are going on and to give them in the affairs that concern us most some measure of intelligent direction. It is not called upon to cherish Utopian notions about the imminence of such intelligent direction of social changes. But it is committed to faith in the possibility of its slow effectuation in the degree in which men realize the full import of the revolution that has already been effected in physical and technical regions.

Wherever the thought of fixity rules, that of all-inclusive unity rules also. The popular philosophy of life is filled with desire to attain such an all-embracing unity, and formal philosophies have been devoted to an intellectual fulfillment of the desire. Consider the place occupied in popular thought by search for *the* meaning of life and *the* purpose of the universe. Men who look for a single purport and a single end either frame an idea of them according to their private desires and tradition, or else, not finding any such single unity, give up in despair and conclude that there is no genuine meaning and value in any of life's episodes.

The alternatives are not exhaustive, however. There is no need of deciding between no meaning at all and one single, all-embracing meaning. There are many meanings and many purposes in the situations with which we are confronted — one, so to say, for each situation. Each offers its own challenge to thought and endeavor, and presents its own potential value.

It is impossible, I think, even to begin to imagine the changes that would come into life — personal and collective — if the idea of a plurality of interconnected meanings and purposes replaced that of *the* meaning and purpose. Search for a single, inclusive good is doomed to failure. Such happiness as life is capable of comes from the full participation of all our powers in the endeavor to wrest from each changing situation of experience its own full and unique meaning. Faith in the varied possibilities of diversified experience is attended with the joy of constant discovery and of constant growing. Such a joy is possible even in the midst of trouble and defeat, whenever life-experiences are treated as potential disclosures of meanings and values that are to be used as means to a fuller and more significant future experience. Belief in a single purpose distracts thought and wastes energy that would help make the world better if it were directed to attainable ends.

IV

I have stated a general principle, because philosophy, I take it, is more than

an enumeration of items of belief with respect to this and that question. But the principle can acquire definiteness only in application to actual issues. How about religion? Does renunciation of the extra-empirical compel also an abandonment of all religion? It certainly exacts a surrender of that supernaturalism and fixed dogma and rigid institutionalism with which Christianity has been historically associated. But as I read human nature and history, the intellectual content of religions has always finally adapted itself to scientific and social conditions after they have become clear. In a sense, it has been parasitic upon the latter.

For this reason I do not think that those who are concerned about the future of a religious attitude should trouble themselves about the conflict of science with traditional doctrines — though I can understand the perplexity of fundamentalists and liberals alike who have identified religion with a special set of beliefs. Concern about the future of religion should take, I think, a different direction. It is difficult to see how religion, after it has accommodated itself to the disintegrating effect of knowledge upon the dogmas of the church, can accommodate itself to traditional social institutions and remain vital.

It seems to me that the chief danger to religion lies in the fact that it has become so respectable. It has become largely a sanction of what socially exists — a kind of gloss upon institutions and conventions. Primitive Christianity was devastating in its claims. It was a religion of renunciation and denunciation of the "world"; it demanded a change of heart that entailed a revolutionary change in human relationships. Since the Western world is now alleged to be Christianized, a world of outworn institutions is accepted and blessed. A religion that began as a demand for a revolutionary change and that has become a sanction to established economic, political, and international institutions should perhaps lead its sincere devotees to reflect upon the sayings of the one worshiped as its founder: "Woe unto you when all men shall speak well of you," and, "Blessed are ye when men shall revile you and persecute you."

I do not mean by this that the future of religion is bound up with a return to the apocalyptic vision of the speedy coming of a heavenly kingdom. I do not mean that I think early Christianity has within itself even the germs of a ready-made remedy for present ills and a ready-made solution for present problems. Rather I would suggest that the future of religion is connected with the possibility of developing a faith in the possibilities of human experience and human relationships that will create a vital sense of the solidarity of human interests and inspire action to make that sense a reality. If our nominally religious institutions learn how to use their symbols and rites to express and enhance such a faith, they may become useful allies of a conception of life that is in harmony with knowledge and social needs.

Since existing Western civilization is what it is so largely because of the forces of industry and commerce, a genuinely religious attitude will be concerned with all that deeply affects human work and the leisure that is dependent upon the conditions and results of work. That is, it will acknowledge the significance of economic factors in life instead of evading the issue. The greatest obstacle that exists to the apprehension and actualization of the possibilities of experience is found in our economic regime. One does not have to accept the doctrine of economic determination of history and insti-

tutions to be aware that the opportunities of men in general to engage in an experience that is artistically and intellectually rich and rewarding in the daily modes of human intercourse is dependent upon economic conditions. As long as the supreme effort of those who influence thought and set the conditions under which men act is directed toward maintenance of the existing money economy and private profit, faith in the possibilities of an abundant and significant experience, participated in by all, will remain merely philosophic. While this matter was led up to by a consideration of religion, its significance extends far beyond the matter of religion. It affects every range and aspect of life.

Many persons have become acutely conscious of economic evils as far as they bear upon the life of wage earners, who form the great mass of mankind. It requires somewhat more imagination to see how the experience of those who are, as we say, well-to-do or are "comfortably off" is restricted and distorted. They seem to enjoy the advantages of the present situation. But they suffer as deeply from its defects. The artist and scientific inquirer are pushed outside the main currents of life and become appendages to its fringe or caterers to its injustices. All aesthetic and intellectual interests suffer in consequence. Useless display and luxury, the futile attempt to secure happiness through the possession of things, social position, and economic power over others, are manifestations of the restriction of experience that exists among those who seemingly profit by the present order. Mutual fear, suspicion, and jealously are also its products. All of these things deflect and impoverish human experience beyond all calculation.

There may have been a time when such things had to be endured because mankind had neither the knowledge nor the arts by which to attain an abundant life shared by all. As it becomes increasingly evident that science and technology have given us the resources for dealing effectively with the workings of economic forces, the philosophy of the possibilities of experience takes on concrete meaning.

V

Our international system (since, with all its disorder, it *is* a system) presents another example, writ large, of the restriction of experience created by exclusiveness and isolation. In the arts and technical sciences, there already exist contacts and exchanges undreamed of even a century ago. Barring our execrable tariff walls, the same is true of commerce in physical commodities. But at the same time, race and color prejudice have never had such opportunity as they have now to poison the mind, while nationalism is elevated into a religion called patriotism. Peoples and nations exist in a state of latent antagonism when not engaged in overt conflict. This state of affairs narrows and impoverishes the experience of every individual in countless ways. An outward symbol of this restriction is found in the oft cited fact that eighty per cent of our national expenditure goes to pay for the results of past wars and preparing for future wars. The conditions of a vitally valuable experience for the individual are so bound up with complex, collective, social relationships that the individualism of the past has lost its meaning. Individuals will always be the center and the consummation of experience, but what an individual actually *is* in his life-experience depends upon the nature and movement of associated life. This is the lesson enforced by both our economic and our international systems.

Morals is not a theme by itself because it is not an episode nor department by itself. It marks the issue of all the converging forces of life. Codes that set up fixed and unchanging ends and rules have necessarily relaxed in the face of changing science and society. A new and effective morale can emerge only from an exploration of the realities of human association. Psychology and the social disciplines are beginning to furnish the instrumentalities of this inquiry. In no field has disrespect for experience had more disastrous consequences, for in no other has there been such waste. The experience of the past is largely thrown away. There has been no deliberate, cumulative process, no systematic transmission of what is learned in the contacts and intercourse of individuals with one another. It has been thought enough to hand on fixed rules and fixed ends. Controlled moral progress can begin only where there is the sifting and communication of the results of all relevant experiences of human association, such as now exists as a matter of course in the experiences of science with the natural world.

In popular speech, morals usually signifies matters of sex relationship. Phenomena of a period of acute transition like those of the present are poor material upon which to base prediction and foresight. But it is clear that the codes which still nominally prevail are the result of one-sided and restricted conditions. Present ideas of love, marriage, and the family are almost exclusively masculine constructions. Like all idealizations of human interests that express a dominantly one-sided experience, they are romantic in theory and prosaic in operation. Sentimental idealization on one side has its obverse in a literally conceived legal system. The realities of the relationships of men, women, and children to one another have been submerged in this fusion of sentimentalism and legalism. The growing freedom of women can hardly have any other outcome than the production of more realistic and more human morals. It will be marked by a new freedom, but also by a new severity. For it will be enforced by the realities of associated life as they are disclosed to careful and systematic inquiry, and not by a combination of convention and an exhausted legal system with sentimentality.

VI

The chief intellectual characteristic of the present age is its despair of any constructive philosophy — not just in its technical meaning, but in the sense of any integrated outlook and attitude. The developments of the last century have gone so far that we are now aware of the shock and overturn in older beliefs. But the formation of a new, coherent view of nature and man based upon facts consonant with science and actual social conditions is still to be had. What we call the Victorian Age seemed to have such a philosophy. It was a philosophy of hope, of progress, of all that is called liberalism. The growing sense of unsolved social problems, accentuated by the war, has shaken our faith. It is impossible to recover its mood.

The result is disillusionment about all comprehensive and positive ideas. The possession of constructive ideals is taken to be an admission that one is living in a realm of fantasy. We have lost confidence in reason because we have learned that man is chiefly a creature of habit and emotion. The notion that habit and impulse can themselves be rendered intelligent on any large and social scale is felt to be only another illusion. Because the hopes and expectations of the past

have been discredited, there is cynicism as to all far-reaching plans and policies. That the very knowledge which enables us to detect the illusory character of past hopes and aspirations — a knowledge denied those who held them — may enable us to form purposes and expectations that are better grounded, is overlooked.

In fact, the contrast with the optimism of the Victorian Age is significant of the need and possibility of a radically different type of philosophy. For that era did not question the essential validity of older ideas. It recognized that the new science demanded a certain purification of traditional beliefs — such, for example, as the elimination of the supernatural. But in the main, Victorian thought conceived of new conditions as if they merely put in our hands effective instruments for realizing old ideals. The shock and uncertainty so characteristic of the present marks the discovery that the older ideals themselves are undermined. Instead of science and technology giving us better means for bringing them to pass, they are shaking our confidence in all large and comprehensive beliefs and purposes.

Such a phenomenon is, however, transitory. The impact of the new forces is for the time being negative. Faith in the divine author and authority in which Western civilization confided, inherited ideas of the soul and its destiny, of fixed revelation, of completely stable institutions, of automatic progress, have been made impossible for the cultivated mind of the Western world. It is psychologically natural that the outcome should be a collapse of faith in all fundamental organizing and directive ideas. Skepticism becomes the mark and even the pose of the educated mind. It is the more influential because it is no longer directed against this and that article of the older creeds but is rather a bias against any kind of far-reaching ideas, and a denial of systematic participation on the part of such ideas in the intelligent direction of affairs.

It is in such a context that a thoroughgoing philosophy of experience, framed in the light of science and technique, has its significance. For it, the breakdown of traditional ideas is an opportunity. The possibility of producing the kind of experience in which science and the arts are brought unitedly to bear upon industry, politics, religion, domestic life, and human relations in general, is itself something novel. We are not accustomed to it even as an idea. But faith in it is neither a dream nor a demonstrated failure. It is a faith. Realization of the faith, so that we may work in larger measure by sight of things achieved, is in the future. But the conception of it as a possibility when it is worked out in a coherent body of ideas, critical and constructive, forms a philosophy, an organized attitude of outlook, interpretation, and construction. A philosophic faith, being a tendency to action, can be tried and tested only in action. I know of no viable alternative in the present day to such a philosophy as has been indicated.

John Dewey: WHAT I BELIEVE, *Revised*

MY contribution to the first series of essays in *Living Philosophies* put forward the idea of faith in the possibilities of experience as the heart of my own philosophy. In the course of that contribution I said, "Individuals will always be the center and the consummation of experience, but what the individual actually *is* in his life experience depends upon the nature and movement of associated life." I have not changed my faith in experience nor my belief that individuality is its center and consummation. But there has been a change in emphasis. I should now wish to emphasize more than I formerly did that individuals are the finally decisive factors of the nature and movement of associated life.

The cause of this shift of emphasis is the events of the intervening years. The rise of dictatorships and totalitarian states and the decline of democracy have been accompanied with loud proclamation of the idea that only the state, the political organization of society, can give security to individuals. In return for the security thus obtained, it is asserted even more loudly (and with much greater practical effect) that individuals owe everything to the state.

This fundamental challenge compels all who believe in liberty and democracy to rethink the whole question of the relation of individual choice, belief, and action to institutions; to reflect on the kind of social changes that will make individuals in actuality the centers and the possessors of worth-while experience. In re-thinking this issue in the light of the rise of totalitarian states, I am led to emphasize the idea that only the voluntary initiative and voluntary co-operation of individuals can produce social institutions that will protect the liberties necessary for achieving development of genuine individuality.

This change of emphasis does not in any way minimize the belief that the ability of individuals to develop genuine individuality is intimately connected with the social conditions under which they associate with one another. But it attaches fundamental importance to the activities of individuals in determining the social conditions under which they live. It has been shown in the last few years that democratic *institutions* are no guarantee for the existence of democratic individuals. The alternative is that individuals who prize their own liberties and who prize the liberties of other individuals, individuals who are democratic in thought and action, are the sole final warrant for the existence and endurance of democratic institutions.

The belief that the voluntary activities of individuals in voluntary association with one another is the only basis of democratic institutions does not mean a return to the older philosophy of individualism. That philosophy thought of the individual after the analogy of older physical science. He was taken to be a center without a field. His relations to other individuals were as mechanical and external as those of Newtonian atoms to one another. Liberty was supposed to be automatically acquired by abolition of restraints and constraints; all the individual needed was to be let alone.

The negative and empty character of this individualism had consequences which produced a reaction toward an equally arbitrary and one-sided collectivism. This reaction is identical with the rise of the new form of political despotism. The decline of democracy and the rise of authoritarian states which claim they can do for individuals what the latter cannot by any possibility do for themselves are the two sides of one and the same indivisible picture.

Political collectivism is now marked in all highly industrialized countries, even when it does not reach the extreme of the totalitarian state. It is the social consequence of the development of private capitalistic collectivism in industry and finance. For this reason those who look backward to restoration of the latter system are doomed to fight a losing battle. For the tendency toward state socialism and state capitalism is the product of the economic collectivism of concentrated capital and labor that was produced by mass production and mass distribution. The inherent identity of the two forms of collectivism is disguised by the present angry and clamorous controversy waged between representatives of private and public collectivism, both claiming to speak, moreover, in the interest of the individual, one for his initiative, the other for his security.

The strict reciprocity that exists between the two collectivisms is also covered from view because they are promoted in the respective interests of different social groups. Roughly speaking, the "haves" stand for private collectivism and the "have nots" for state collectivism. The bitter struggle waged between them in the political arena conceals from recognition the fact that both favor some sort of collectivism and represent complementary aspects of the same total picture.

Between the struggles of the two parties, both purporting to serve the cause of ultimate individual freedom, the individual has in fact little show and little opportunity. Bewildered and temporarily lost anyway, the din of the contending parties increases his bewilderment. Everything is so big that he wants to ally himself with bigness, and he is told that he must make his choice between big industry and finance and the big national political state. For a long time, what political agencies did and did not do in legislation and in the courts favored the growth of private capitalistic collectivism. By way of equalizing conditions, I do not doubt that for some time to come political activity will move in the direction of support of underprivileged groups who have been oppressed and made insecure by the growth of concentrated industry and finance. The imminent danger, as events of recent years demonstrate, is that political activity will attempt to retrieve the balance by moving in the direction of state socialism.

Indeed, many persons will ask how it is possible for political action to restore the balance except by direct control over and even ownership of big industrial and financial enterprises. The answer in general is that political activity can, first and foremost, engage in aggressive maintenance of the civil liberties of free speech, free publication and intercommunication, and free assemblage. In the second place, the government can do much to encourage and promote in a positive way the growth of a great variety of voluntary co-operative undertakings.

This promotion involves abolition or drastic modification of a good many institutions that now have political support, since they stand in the way of effective voluntary association for social ends. There are tariffs and other monopoly-furthering devices that keep back individual initiative and voluntary co-opera-

tion. There is our system of land tenure and taxation that puts a premium on the holding of land — including all natural resources — for the sake of private profit in a way that effectively prevents individuals from access to the instruments of individual freedom. There is the political protection given to return on long-term capital investments which are not now accompanied by any productive work, and which are, therefore, a direct tax levied on the productive work of others: an almost incalculable restriction, in its total effect, upon individual freedom.

The intrinsic likeness of political and private collectivism is shown in the fact that the government has had recourse to promotion of a regime of scarcity instead of increased productivity. It is evident on its face that enforced restriction of productivity, whether enforced in the name of private profit or of public relief, can have only a disastrous effect, directly and indirectly, upon individual freedom. But given existing conditions, it is the sole alternative to governmental activity that would abolish such limitations upon voluntary action as have been mentioned, a list that would easily be made more specific and more extensive.

Moreover, the principle of confining political action to policies that provide the conditions for promoting the voluntary association of free individuals does not limit governmental action to negative measures. There are, for example, such political activities as are now represented by provision of public highways, public schools, protection from fire, etc., etc., supported by taxation. This type of activity can doubtless be extended in a way which will release individual liberties instead of restricting them. The principle laid down does not deter political activity from engaging in constructive measures. But it does lay down a criterion by which every political proposal shall be judged: Does it tend definitely in the direction of increase of voluntary, free choice and activity on the part of individuals?

The danger at present, as I have already said, is that in order to get away from the evils of private economic collectivism we shall plunge into political economic collectivism. The danger is so great that the course that has been suggested will be regarded as an unrealistic voice crying in the wilderness. It would be unrealistic to make light of the present drive in the direction of state socialism. But it is even more unrealistic to overlook the dangers involved in taking the latter course. For the events of recent years have demonstrated that state capitalism leads toward the totalitarian state whether of the Russian or the Fascist variety.

We now have demonstrations of the consequences of two social movements. Earlier events proved that private economic collectivism produced social anarchy, mitigated by the control exercised by an oligarchic group. Recent events have shown that state socialism or public collectivism leads to suppression of everything that individuality stands for. It is not too late for us in this country to learn the lessons taught by these two great historic movements. The way is open for a movement which will provide the fullest opportunity for co-operative voluntary endeavor. In this movement political activity will have a part, but a subordinate one. It will be confined to providing the conditions, both negative and positive, that favor the voluntary activity of individuals.

There is, however, a socialism which is not state socialism. It may be called functional socialism. Its nature may be illustrated by the movement for socialization of medicine. I think this socialization is bound to come anyway. But it may come about in two very different ways. It may come into existence as a state measure, under political control; or it may come about as the result of the efforts of the medical profession made aware of its social function and its responsibilities. I cannot develop the significance of the illustration. But as an illustration, its significance applies to all occupational groups; that is, to all groups that are engaged in any form of socially useful, productive, activity.

The technocrats of recent memory had a glimpse of the potentialities inherent in self-directed activities of autonomous groups performing necessary social functions. But they ruined their vision when they fell into the pit dug by Wells and Shaw, that of rule from above by an elite of experts — although according to technocracy engineers were to be the samurai. The N.I.R.A. had a glimpse of self-governing industrial groups. But, quite apart from its conflict with the existing legal system, the plan loaded the dice in favor of the existing system of control of industry — with a few sops thrown in to "labor." At best it could not have worked out in the direction of freely functioning occupational groups. The Marxists professed the idea, but they held it as an ultimate goal to be realized through seizure of political power by a single class, the proletariat. The withering away of the state which was supposed to take place is not in evidence. On the contrary, seizure of political power as the means to the ultimate end of free individuals organized in functional occupational groups has led to the production of one more autocratic political state.

The dialectic that was supposed to work in solving the contradiction between increase of political power and its abolition is conspicuous by its absence — and inherently so. The Fascists also proclaim the idea of a corporate state. But again there is reliance upon uncontrolled and irresponsible political power. Instead of a corporate society of functional groups there is complete suppression of every formal voluntary association of individuals.

Before concluding that in America adoption of the method of voluntary effort in voluntary associations of individuals with one another is hopeless, one should observe the course of history. For if history teaches anything it is that judgments regarding the future have been predicated upon the basis of the tendencies that are most conspicuous at the time, while in fact the great social changes which have produced new social institutions have been the cumulative effect of flank movements that were not obvious at the time of their origin.

During the height of expanding competitive industrialism, for example, it was freely predicted that its effect would be a future society of free individuals and of free nations so interdependent that lasting peace would be achieved — *vide* Herbert Spencer. Now that the actual result has been the opposite, it is prophe- sied on the basis of the tendencies that are now most prominent that increased control of industrial activity by the state will usher in an era of abundance and security. Nevertheless those who can escape the hypnotic influence exercised by the immediate contemporary scene are aware that movements going on in the interstices of the existing order are those which will in fact shape the future. As a friend of mine puts it, the last thing the lord of the feudal castle would have imagined was that the future of society was with the forces that were represented by the humble trader who set up his post under the walls of his castle.

I am not optimistic enough to believe that voluntary associations of individuals, which are even now building up within the cracks of a crumbling social order, will speedily reverse the tendency toward political collectivism. But I am confident that the ultimate way out of the present social dead end lies with the movement these associations are initiating. Individuals who have not lost faith in themselves and in other individuals will increasingly ally themselves with these groups. Sooner or later they will construct the way out of present confusion and conflict. The sooner it is done the shorter will be the time of chaos and catastrophe.

Lewis Mumford:

THE PRAGMATIC ACQUIESCENCE

THE Civil War arose in a mess of muddy issues. The abolitionists' attack upon slavery, full of moral righteousness and oblivious to the new varieties of slavery that were being practiced under industrialism, stiffened the South into a spasm even more self-righteous, even more blind. Twenty years of fierce debate found the Southerner frequently denying that the Negro was a human being: it also found the abolitionist denying that the slaveholder was a human being. In that temper, all the rational humane people who were searching for effective measures to reduce the area of slavery and pension off the institution found their hands tied and their throats throttled. The South fought to preserve slavery by extending its territory: the answer to this was natural: and then, to muddle matters worse, the issue was mixed up with Centralism versus State's Rights. There were honest abolitionists who desired that the Union should break up into a Slave State and a Free State which would serve as a biblical city of refuge; there were slavery men who were reluctant to see the Union destroyed.

The smoke of warfare blinded the issue further. When it cleared away, the slave question had disappeared but the "Negro question" remained; and in the inevitable dictatorship of war, the central government, particularly the Executive, emerged, mystically raising aloft the Union as a mask for all its depredations. What the office-holders in the central government called "the menace of sectionalism," and what we may call equally "the promise of regionalism" was exterminated for fully two generations. Local life declined. The financial centers grew: through the mechanism of finance, New York and Chicago began to dominate the rest of the country. Presently the novel of "local color" appeared — proof enough that the color had washed out.

The Civil War cut a white gash through the history of the country; it dramatized in a stroke the changes that had begun to take place during the preceding twenty or thirty years. On one side lay the Golden Day, the period of an Elizabethan daring on the sea, of a well-balanced adjustment of farm and factory in the East, of a thriving regional culture, operating through the lecture-lyceum and the provincial college; an age in which the American mind had flourished and had begun to find itself. When the curtain rose on the post-bellum scene, this old America was for all practical purposes demolished: industrialism had entered overnight, had transformed the practices of agriculture, had encouraged a mad exploitation of mineral oil, natural gas, and coal, and had made the unscrupulous master of finance, fat with war-profits, the central figure of the situation. All the crude practices of British paleotechnic industry appeared on the new scene without relief or mitigation.

On both sides of the line many a fine lad had died in battle, and those who survived, in more subtle ways died, too.

Some of them had evaded the opportunity for physical death: Mark Twain, after a brief anomalous period in the army, ran away to Nevada, William Dean Howells accepted a consular post in Venice, Stanley Hall, honest enough to record the point in his autobiography, accepted the services of a paid substitute. Happy the dead! The period after the war was the Gilded Age, with a vengeance. Sidney Lanier, who had served the South, and emerged a skeleton, faced the bitter truth of this great outburst of material enterprise:

> Trade is trade but sings a lie:
> 'Tis only war grown miserly.

Unchecked, unmodified, industrialism controlled the mind as well as the material apparatus of the country: men who had a cut for scholarship, like Charles Francis Adams, became railroad magnates, and the son of the Great Emancipator became the head of the Pullman Corporation. H. G. Eastman founded the business school in 1855, and by the end of the war that which was established in Poughkeepsie had more than a thousand pupils. The Massachusetts Institute of Technology was established in 1861 and dedicated to the practical application of science in the arts, agriculture, manufacture and commerce; when it was opened in 1865 the courses on industrial technology dominated the whole program. The multiplication of these institutes witnessed the new orientation in industry and life. "We do not properly live in these days," one of the early Transcendentalists, J. S. Dwight, had written, "but everywhere, with patent inventions and complex arrangements, are getting ready to live. The end is lost in the means, life is smothered in appliances." The Gilded Age accepted these facts with complacence: business was the only activity it respected; comfort was the only result it sought. Gone were the tragic doubts that had vexed the Transcendentalist and made life interesting and terrible and very beautiful for all the sensitive minds: the steel mill, the mine, the counting house, claimed them; or if not that, they went to an equally materialist post-war Germany, dominated by Bismarck and Krupp, and specialized in their *Fach*, as they might specialize in railroad securities or foreign markets.

One sees the great breach between the two generations in the biographies of fathers and children, in Henry James the elder and his two sons, or, more drastically, in Bronson Alcott and his far more famous daughter Louisa. Alcott, a son of a small Connecticut farmer, got an education peddling "notions" in the plantations of Virginia; and he became both a significant personality, and within the province of education, an interesting thinker: in an age that found Spencer too mystical and difficult, he was a walking embodiment of Plato and Plotinus. Louisa, one of his children, grew up in Bronson's household, worshiped Emerson, and looked upon her father as a well-meaning but silly old man. As a result, the daughter of the philosopher reverted on a lower level to the Yankee peddler: she became a hack writer, purveying lollypops and chocolate cordials to the middle-class market. Her realistic judgment and her bitter, merciless tongue were at the service of a childish fantasy: her fiction took the place in politer circles of the new ten-cent shocker.

Of all Louisa Alcott's books only one has survived for us. It is that which was made possible by the poor and abstemious life her father's silly ways had thrust upon his children in Concord. Little Women was the picture of a happy childhood: that was all: yet it contained so much of what every child had gone through, and so much of what a starved childhood would hope for, that it became universal. Louisa's imagination offered her nothing that she could pit against this memory: with all its scrimping and penury, the reality had been equal to the heart's desire. All America after the war turned to Little Women: and why? Was it not because the only meaning of their life had been in childhood? Maturity had nothing to offer them; it was only before they had started to make a living that they had lived. Boyhood meant home: maturity meant, not a larger home, but exile. Observe that the beam cast by Transcendentalism into the generation that followed was neither Nature nor the Duty of Civil Disobedience nor the Orphic Sayings: no, Transcendentalism said nothing — except that childhood could be happy. That was a recollection that smarted!

Those who were born after 1850 scarcely knew what they were missing; but those who had reached their nonage a little before the great conflict knew it only too well. "How surprised," wrote one of them, "would some of those [Dial] writers be, if they should now in prosaic days read what they then wrote under the spell of that fine frenzy!" "We have found," wrote another, " 'realizing the ideal,' to be impracticable in proportion as the ideal is raised high. But 'idealizing the real,' as I shall maintain, is not only practicable but the main secret of the art of living. . . . There is a wise sentence in the otherwise trifling opera of the 'Grand Duchess' which says, 'If we can't get what we set our hearts on, we must set our hearts on what we can get.' " Excellent worldly wisdom! Doubtless it made one a little more comfortable as one tossed uneasily on one's bed at night, haunted by the ghost of what one might have been.

The post-war generation idealized the real, in its novels, which depicted so much of actual existence as might comfortably be exposed, and in its philosophy, which disclosed so much of the universe as could be assimilated to its feeble desires. As for those who knew better than this, what blighted figures they were — outcasts, almost beyond the pale of humanity, the sad, grim Melville, the proud macabre Bierce. They lived in houses that were dingy wells of darkness; and in the innermost rooms of these houses, cut off from the light in front and the light in the rear, their souls dwelt too, unused to either happy memories or good prospects. "Perhaps you know," wrote Lanier to Bayard Taylor, "that with us of the younger generation in the South since the war, pretty much the whole of life has been merely not dying." That held for the North as well. A good part of their life was merely not dying. Each of the principal literary figures of post-bellum America, Mark Twain, Ambrose Bierce, Henry James, William Dean Howells, William James, was the remains of a man. None was quite able to fill his own shape. They might doubt that a Golden Day had once dawned; but they had only to look around to discover the Gilt of their own. Well might the heroine of Henry Adams's Democracy say: "You grow six inches tall and then you stop. Why will not somebody grow to be a tree and cast a shadow?"

In America's Coming of Age, Mr. Van Wyck Brooks first called attention to the broken rhythm of American life, with its highbrows and lowbrows, its Edwardses and Franklins, its transcendentalists and empiricists. The gap between them widened after the Civil War; for the war left behind a barbarized population which had probably lost more civil habits in four years than the pioneer had in the course of forty. All that was left of Transcendentalism in the Gilded Age was what Howells showed in the hero of A Hazard of New Fortunes — "an inner elegance." The surviving idealist did not, perhaps, particularly believe in the practical work he found himself doing; but he did not believe in anything else sufficiently to cease doing it. In a quite simple and literal sense, he lacked the courage of his convictions: what was even worse, perhaps, was that he never acquired any new convictions that might have given him courage. The post-war generation shows us nature-lovers like John Burroughs but no Thoreaus, schoolmasters like Sanborn and William Harris, but no Alcotts, novelists like Howells, but no Melvilles. It is not hard to define the difference; to put it crudely, the guts of idealism were gone.

The mission of creative thought is to gather into it all the living sources of its day, all that is vital in the practical life, all that is intelligible in science, all that is relevant in the social heritage and, recasting these things into new forms and symbols, to react upon the blind drift of convention and habit and routine. Life flourishes only in this alternating rhythm of dream and deed: when one appears without the other, we can look forward to a shrinkage, a lapse, a devitalization. Idealism is a bad name for this mission; it is just as correct to call it realism; since it is part of the natural history of the human mind. What is valid in idealism is the belief in this process of re-molding, re-forming, re-creating, and so humanizing the rough chaos of existence. That belief had vanished: it no longer seemed a genuine possibility. As Moncure Conway had said: we must idealize the real. There was the work of a Howells, a Clemens, a James. It was an act of grand acquiescence. Transcendentalism, as Emerson caustically said, had resulted in a headache; but the pragmatism that followed it was a paralysis. This generation had lost the power of choice; it bowed to the inevitable; it swam with the tide; and it went as far as the tide would carry it. When Edward Bellamy came to express the utmost of its ambitions, in the utopia called Looking Backward, his mind dwelt lovingly on telephonic broadcasting, upon perfect public restaurants, and upon purchase by sample, as in the mail-order houses — all excellent devices, perhaps, but not in themselves sufficient to stir the mind out of its sluggish acceptance of the blind drift of things. One remembers that a little earlier than Bellamy a certain Danish bishop began to institute the co-operative commonwealth by reviving the folk-ballads of his countrymen.

*   *   *

The Gilded Age tarnished quickly: culture could not flourish in that environment. Those who could not accept their external milieu fled abroad, like Henry James. As for those who remained, perhaps the most significant of all was William James. He gave this attitude of compromise and acquiescence a name: he called it pragmatism: and the name stands not merely for his own philosophy, but for something in which that philosophy was deeply if unconsciously entangled, the spirit of a whole age.

William James, born in 1842, became a philosopher by a long, circuitous route, which began with chemistry, physiology, and medicine, and first flourished in its own right only as the century came to an end. As a youth, he debated over his capacities as an artist, and threw them aside. As a mature mind, he was ridden by an overwhelming interest in philosophy; but for twenty years or more he threw that aside, too. The deflection of his career from his innermost wishes was, one is inclined to think, the outcome of a neurotic conflict, which plagued him as a young man of twenty-eight. Equipped with a cosmopolitan education, and a wide variety of contacts in Europe, James returned to his own soil with the wan longing of an exile. Every time he greeted Europe, apparently, its charms increased his homesickness. He had for America some of the agitated enthusiasm and unguarded receptivity of a convert. He resisted Europe: he accepted America, and though he disliked at times the dusty, meeting-house air of Cambridge, he returned to it, and breathed it, as if it had descended from the mountain tops.

One searches James's pages in vain for a *Weltanschauung*: but one gets an excellent view of America. He had the notion that pragmatism would effect an overturn in philosophy: but the fact was that it killed only what was already dead, the dry, unrelated rationalism of the theologists, or the vacant absolutism of idealists who chose to take the philosophy of Hegel without the concrete history which gave it a rational content. James's lack of a world view was due as much as anything, perhaps, to his positive dread of the difficulties of attaining one. In the crisis of his illness in 1870, under the influence of his newly attained belief in free-will, he wrote: "Not in maxims, not in Anschauungen, but in accumulated *acts* of thought lies salvation." Hence the fragmentary quality of James's philosophy. His supreme act of thought was his Psychology, a book over which he labored for a decade; but though the book is full of discreet wisdom and penetrating observation, carried to the limits of the scientific investigation of his day, James himself was dissatisfied with this act — it had impeded his progress towards Philosophy!

Beside the richness of Emerson's thought, which played over the whole field of existence, James was singularly jejune: he made up for his lack of comprehensive ideas by the brilliance and the whimsical reasonableness of his personality. He divested philosophy of its high hat and its painful white collar, and by the mere force of his presence made it human again. His personality had the curious effect of giving vitality to even moribund ideas; and the superficial reader might easily mix up the full-blooded James with the notions that lived again through this temporary transfusion. He was above all things the psychologist, commenting upon the place of philosophy and religion in the individual life, rather than the thinker, creating the philosophy which should take the place. His pragmatism was — was it not? — an attempt to cut through a personal dilemma and still preserve logical consistency: he wished to retain some surviving representative of the God of his fathers, without throwing over the scientific method in the fields where it had proved valuable. He used philosophy to seek peace, rather than understanding, forgetful of the fact that if peace is all one needs, ale can do more "than Milton can, to justify God's ways to man." I am not sure but that this search for anesthetics may prove in the long run to be the clue to the Nineteenth Century, in all its depauperate phases. The use of ether itself first came as a parlor sport in dull little American communities that had no good wine to bring a milder oblivion from their boredom; and perhaps one may look upon anesthetics in all their physical and spiritual forms — ether, Christian Science, speed — as the culmination of the Protestant attack upon the senses. I throw this out by the way. The fact is that pragmatism *was* a blessed anesthetic.

If one could reconstruct New England in Emerson, one could, I think, recover great tracts of pioneer and industrial America from the pragmatists, the pioneer especially in James, the industrialist in his great pupil, Dewey. James's insistence upon the importance of novelty and freshness echoes on a philosophic plane the words of Mark Twain. "What is it that confers the noblest delight? . . . Discovery! To know that you are walking where no others have walked, that you are beholding what human eye has not seen before; that you are breathing virgin atmosphere. To give birth to an idea — to discover a great thought. . . . To find a new planet, to invent a new hinge, to find the way to make the lightning carry your message. To be the *first* — that is the idea." James's opposition to a block universe, his notion that salvation had to be worked out, his feeling that there was no savor, no excitement, no interest "in following the good path if we do not feel that evil is also possible and natural, nay, threatening and imminent" — what was all this, too, but the animus of the pioneer, translated into dialectic?

I do not say this to belittle James's interest in these notions: a philosophy must, plainly, grow out of an experience of life, and the feeling of boundless possibility that springs from James's pages was one of the healthy influences of the frontier. The point is, however, that a valuable philosophy must take into account a greater range of experiences than the dominating ones of a single generation; it is good to include these, but if it includes only these, it is still in a state of cultural adolescence. It is the remote and the missing that the philosopher

must be ready to supply: the Spartan element in Plato's Republic was not familiar or genial to the Athenian temperament; but in the dry-rot of Athenian democracy it was the one element that might have restored it, and Plato went outside his familiar ground to take account of it and supply it. In Europe, James's influence has proved, I think, invigorating; for European philosophy had assimilated no such experiences as the frontier offered, and the pluralism and free-mindedness of James provided a release from a too cut-and-dried universe of discourse.

In America, however, James was only warming over again in philosophy the hash of everyday experience in the Gilded Age: he did not make a fresh combination, or a new application of these experiences; he was the reporter, rather than the creator. James's most important contribution to metaphysics was possibly his technical analysis of radical empiricism, which put relations and abstract qualities on the same plane as physical objects or the so-called external world: both were given in experience. But the totality of James's philosophy has to-day chiefly an illustrative value: woe to the seeker who tries to live by it, or find in it the key to a reasonable existence. The new ideas that James achieved were not so influential as those he accepted and rested upon; and the latter, pretty plainly, were the protestantism, the individualism, the scientific distrust of "values," which had come down in unbroken succession from Calvin and Luther, from Locke and Hobbes and Hume and Bentham and Mill.

James referred to pragmatism as "an alteration in the 'seat of authority' that reminds one of the protestant reformation. And as, to papal minds, protestantism has often seemed a mere mess of anarchy and confusion, such, no doubt, will pragmatism seem to ultra-rationalist minds in philosophy. . . . But life wags on all the same, and compasses its ends, in protestant countries. I venture to think that philosophic protestantism will compass a not dissimilar prosperity." How curious was James's illusion that life was compassing its ends! That was just the point: that was what any one with a sense of history was forced to doubt when he contemplated the "prosperity" of Manchester, Essen, Glasgow, Lille, or Pittsburgh: life, distinctly, was not compassing its ends, and all the boasting and self-gratulation in the world could not hide the fact that something was wrong, not just in particulars, but with the whole scheme of existence. The particulars were all right in their place: men must delve and spin and weave and smelt and fetch and carry and build; but once these things get out of place, and, instead of ministering to life, limit all its functions, the ends for which life exists are not being compassed. The very words James used to recommend pragmatism should make us suspicious of its pretensions.

"For my part," cried William James, "I do not know what sweat and blood, what the tragedy of this life means except just this: if life is not a struggle in which by success, there is something gained on behalf of the universe, then it is no more than idle amusement." What is this universe which gains something by man's conflict? Is it not, perhaps, like the concept of "the country" which gains virtue by a boy scout's doing one good turn per day? The Hindu *guru*, the Platonic philosopher, aloof from this struggle, is not virtuous in James's sense; neither is the pure scientist, the Clerk-Maxwell, the Faraday, the Gibb, the Einstein — the activity of all these creatures, what is it but "idle amusement?"

James's half-lost and half-redeemed universe satisfied the combative instincts: but life would still be amusing and significant were every vexatious devil banished, were every thorn plucked, were every mosquito exterminated! To find significance only in the fight, in the "action," was the signal of boredom: significant action is either the exercise of a natural function, or activity towards an end. It was the temper of James's mind, and it is the temper of protestantism generally, to take more pleasure in the obstacles than in the achievement. It has the courage to face danger and disaster: this is its great quality: but it has not the courage to face prosperity. In short, protestantism triumphs in a crisis; but it is tempted to prolong the crisis in order to perpetuate the triumph. A humane life does not demand this digging and dogging at the universe; it prospers as well in Eden as it does in the rorty wilderness outside. Growth, development, and reproduction are not categories of the battlefield.

With all the preoccupations fostered by the Gilded Age, which were handed down to the succeeding generation, it was inevitable, I think, that James's ideas should have been caricatured. His doctrine of the verification of judgment, as something involved in the continuous process of thinking, instead of a pre-existent correspondence between truth and reality, was distorted in controversy into a belief in the gospel of getting on. The carefully limited area he left to religious belief in The Will-to-Believe was transformed by ever-so-witty colleagues into the Will-to-Make-Believe. His conscious philosophy of pragmatism, which sought to ease one of the mighty, recurrent dilemmas of his personal life, was translated into a belief in the supremacy of cash-values and practical results; and the man who was perhaps one of the most cosmopolitan and cultivated minds of his generation was treated at times as if he were a provincial writer of newspaper platitudes, full of the gospel of smile.

On the surface, these reactions betrayed little more than the ingrained bias of James's academic colleagues; and yet, as I say, the caricature was almost inevitable, and in his persistent use of financial metaphors he was himself not a little responsible for it. James's thought was permeated with the smell of the Gilded Age: one feels in it the compromises, the evasions, the desire for a comfortable resting place. Getting on was certainly never in James's mind, and cash values did not engross even his passing attention; but, given his milieu, they were what his words reënforced in the habits of the people who gave themselves over to his philosophy. Personally, he was "against all big organizations as such, national ones first and foremost; and against all big successes and big results"; but there was nothing in his philosophy that necessitated these beliefs in his followers.

An English friend of mine used to say that the old-fashioned London banker was often, like Lord Avebury, a financier and a cultivated man: the second generation usually remained good financiers, but had no interest in art or science; the third generation were complete duffers, and good for neither activity. Something like this happened with the pragmatists. There is an enormous distance between William James and the modern professors who become employees in advertising agencies, or bond salesmen, or publicity experts, without any sense of professional degradation; but the line that

connects them is a fairly clear one. Of James one may say with sorrow that he built much worse than he knew. There was still in his personality a touch of an older and honester America — the America of Emerson and of Henry James, Senior, the America that had overthrown the old aristocracies so that every man might claim his place as an aristocrat. But the generation for whom James wrote lived in the dregs of the Gilded Age; and it was not these remoter flavors of personality that they enjoyed. As one comes to James to-day, one is touched by the spectacle of a fine personality, clipped and halted in its flight. As for his philosophy, one cannot doubt that it worked. What one doubts is whether the results of this work were valuable.

It was those who stood outside the circle of the Gilded Age that have, within the last ten or fifteen years, come to seem more important than the dominating figures: Albert Pinkham Ryder in painting, Emily Dickinson in poetry, and Charles Peirce in philosophy. The overtones of the pioneering experience or the industrial scramble were absent for the most part in Peirce's writings; it was for that reason, quite as much as for their technical precision, that they remained unpopular. Peirce was not disrupted by the compromises and shifts of the Gilded Age: he lived his own life, and made none. As a philosopher, he thought deeply about logic, science, history, and the values that ennoble life; and his philosophy was what his own age deeply needed. It has remained for Professor Morris Cohen, in our own time, to resurrect his papers and to discover how fresh and appropriate they are, almost two generations after the first of them was published. Peirce had no part in the pragmatic acquiescence. His voice was a lonely protest. He was lost between two circles: the pragmatists, who were dominated, in Mr. Santayana's excellent phrase, by the foreground; and another group, equally pragmatic, equally a product of the Gilded Age, which was searching for a background. It is these latter who sought, in their own way, to fill up the vacancy that pragmatism left. William James belonged to one group; Henry James to the other; and the America after 1900 was largely the spiritual heir of one or another of these remarkable brothers.

*   *   *

Among the group of New Englanders established in Chicago at the beginning of the century, Mr. John Dewey was perhaps the most distinguished. Among all the writers of this milieu and period, he expressed in his philosophy something more than the mere welter of existence. From the beginning Mr. Dewey was bracketed with William James as one of the founders and developers of pragmatism, or as he himself preferred to call it, instrumentalism; but, in spite of similarities of approach, there were differences between these men which at bottom reflected the intervening of almost a generation between the birth of James and that of Dewey.

William James had a style. Dreiser, Dewey, the commanding writers of the early Chicago school, were at one on this point: they had no style: they wrote in a language which, however concrete its objects, was as fuzzy and formless as lint. There is a homely elegance in James's writing, a beauty in the presentation of the thought, even if the concept of beauty was absent from his philosophy; in the earlier writing of Dewey, on the other hand, one looks in vain for either the concept or its literary equivalent. The come-

down is serious. Style is the indication of a happy mental rhythm, as a firm grip and a red cheek are of health. Lack of style is a lack of organic connection: Dreiser's pages are as formless as a dumpheap: Mr. Dewey's pages are as depressing as a subway ride — they take one to one's destination, but a little the worse for wear. Mr. Randolph Bourne once characterized this quality of Mr. Dewey's mind as "protective coloration"; and the phrase is accurate enough if one means that the creature has identified himself in shape and color with his environment. No one has plumbed the bottom of Mr. Dewey's philosophy who does not feel in back of it the shapelessness, the faith in the current go of things, and the general utilitarian idealism of Chicago — the spirit which produced the best of the early skyscrapers, the Chicago exposition, Burnham's grandiose city plan, the great park and playground system, the clotted disorder of interminable slums, and the vitality of a handful of experimental schools.

Mr. Dewey's philosophy represents what is still positive and purposeful in that limited circle of ideas in which the American mind was originally born; he is at home in the atmosphere of protestantism, with its emphasis upon the role of intelligence in morals; in science, with its emphasis upon procedure, technique, and deliberate experiment; and he embraces technology with the same esthetic faith that Mr. Henry Ford embraces it. Above all, Mr. Dewey believes in democracy; that was at the bottom of his many acceptances of the milieu; what had been produced by the mass of men must somehow be right, and must somehow be more significant than the interests which occupy only a minority! In Mr. Dewey the American mind completed, as it were, its circle, and returned to its origin, amplifying, by the experience of a century, the essential interests of an Edwards, a Franklin, a Paine.

To the things that stand outside this circle of ideas, Mr. Dewey has been essentially antagonistic, or at least unsympathetic. He has been a severe and just critic of conventional education; and he has undermined conceptions of philosophy, art, and religion which represented merely the mummified experiences and aims of other generations: but his criticisms have been conducted with an unqualified belief in the procedures of common sense and technology, because these procedures have led to practical "results." Happiness, too, for him "is found only in success; but success means succeeding, getting forward, moving in advance. It is an active process, not a passive outcome." That is quite another definition of happiness than the equilibrium, the point of inner rest, which the mystic, for example, seeks; but for Mr. Dewey a less active kind of happiness always tends to be "totally separated from renewal of the spirit." In other words, happiness means for Mr. Dewey what it meant for the pioneer: a preparation for something else. He scarcely can conceive that activity may follow the mode of the circle or the pendulum, rather than the railroad train.

In spite of all these opacities, it would be absurd to ignore the great service that instrumentalism has performed; for it has crystallized in philosophic form one of the great bequests of science and modern technology: the respect for coöperative thinking and for manual activity — experiment and invention — in guiding and controlling this process. The notion that action by itself was undignified and foreign to the life of the mind was, of course, a leisure class superstition. Creative thought is not a polite shuffling of observations, memories, and *a priori* logic: that is but one phase of the whole process: man thinking is not a spectatorial "mind" but a completely operative human organism, using in various degrees and at various stages every part of his organism, down to his viscera, and every available form of tool, from the finger which might trace a geometrical theorem in the sand to the logarithm table or the electric furnace. The otiose, leisure-class notion of thinking is that it is the reflection of what one reads in a book or gets by hearsay from other people: the great achievement of the scientific method was to supplant the scholar's chair — which does in fact peculiarly serve one phase of the thinking-process — by the work of the field and the laboratory, by exploration, observation, mechanical contrivance, exact measurement, and coöperative intercourse. With the introduction of the scientific method, men began to think consciously as whole human beings: the worker, the rambler, the traveler, the explorer, enlarged the scope of the mind. If this movement was accompanied by some loss, perhaps, in that part of the thinking process covered by dialectics, the gain was nevertheless a great one.

Mr. Dewey seized upon this achievement and brought out its significance admirably. Its implications should not be neglected. According to Dewey, thought is not mature until it has passed into action: the falsity of philosophy is that it has frequently dealt with ideas which have no such issue, while the weakness of the practical world is that its actions are unintelligent routine, the issue of an unreflective procedure. Action is not opposed to ideas: the means are not one thing, and the final result of attending to them quite another: they are not kitchen maids and parlor guests, connected only by being in the same house. Means which do not lead to significant issues are illiberal and brutal; issues which do not take account of the means necessary to fulfill them are empty and merely "well-meaning." A transcendental-ism which takes such high ground poor humanity cannot stand on it, or an em-piricism which takes such low ground that it introduces no excellence into brute existence — both these things are inimical to life, and absurd — and it has been Mr. Dewey's great merit to point out this absurdity, and so open the way to a more complete kind of activity, in which facts and values, actualities and desires, achieve an active and organic unity.

In its flexibility, in its experimental-ism, in its emphasis upon the ineptitude of any finality, except that involved in the process of living itself, with the per-petual intercourse between the organism and its implicated environment, Mr. Dewey's philosophy expresses a continu-ously formative part of our American experience. For the European, roughly speaking, history is what prevents any-thing new or fresh from being done. It needed the dislocation of settling a New World to discover a to-morrow not actu-ally given in a host of yesterdays. In so far as Mr. Dewey has given expression to these things, his work has been to the good: it is not that flexibility and experi-ment are good in themselves: there are times when it is necessary to be as stiff as a ramrod and as dogmatic as a Scotch dominie — but these things represent a genuine addition to the European experi-ence of life, and to introduce them as categories in philosophy is to extend its boundaries.

The deficiencies of Mr. Dewey's phi-losophy are the deficiences of the Ameri-can scene itself: they arise out of his too easy acceptance of the Seventeenth and Eighteen Century framework of ideas; and although he has written about the influence of Darwinism on philosophy, and has done some of his best work in enriching the concepts of philosophy with biological illustrations and clues, he has not been sufficiently critical of the doctrines and writers whose works lean closest to his own habits of thinking. The utilitarian type of personality has been for the instrumentalist a thoroughly agreeable one: I recollect eulogies of Bacon in Mr. Dewey's works, but none of Shakespeare; appreciations of Locke, but not of Milton; of Bentham, but not Shelley and Keats and Wordsworth and Blake. The thinkers who saw social wel-fare as the principal object of existence, and who naïvely defined it in terms of man's control over the externalities of his environment, through the employment of science and technology, have been nearest to Mr. Dewey's heart. He has even written as if the telephone did away with the necessity for imaginative reverie — as if the imagination itself were just a weak and ineffectual substitute for the more tangible results of invention!

This aspect of Mr. Dewey's instru-mentalism is bound up with a certain democratic indiscriminateness in his per-sonal standards: a Goodyear and a Morse seem to him as high in the scale of hu-man development as a Whitman and a Tolstoi: a rubber raincoat is perhaps a finer contribution to human life than "Wind, Rain, Speed." What indeed is his justification for art? Let him answer in his own words. "Fine art, consciously undertaken as such, is peculiarly instru-mental in quality. It is a device in experi-mentation, carried on for the sake of edu-cation. It exists for the sake of a special-ized use, use being a training of new modes of perception. The creators of such works are entitled, when successful, to the gratitude that we give to inventors of microscopes and microphones; in the end they open new objects to be observed and enjoyed." This is a fairly back-handed eulogy, unless one remembers Mr. Dewey's intense gratitude for all mechanical instruments.

In a similar mood, Mr. Dewey speaks of the "intrinsic worth of invention"; but the point is, of course, that except for the inventor, who is *ipso facto* an artist, the invention is good for what it leads to, whereas a scene in nature, a picture, a poem, a dance, a beautiful conception of the universe, are good for what they are. A well-designed machine may also have the same kind of esthetic value: but the independent joy it gives to the keen mechanic or engineer is not the purpose of its design: whereas art has no other purpose; and when a Duchamps-Villon or a Man Ray wants to create the esthetic equivalent of a machine, he does not employ an engineer, but goes through the same process he would undergo to model the figure of a man. Esthetic enjoyment will often lead to other things, and it is all the happier for doing this: the scene in nature may lead to the planting of a park, the dance may promote physical health: but the essential criterion of art is that it is good without these specific instrumental results, good as a *mode of life*, good as a beatitude. An intelligent life, without these beatitudes, would still be a poor one: the fact that Bentham could mention pushpins in the same breath as poetry shows the deeply anesthetic and life-denying quality of the utilitarian philosophy.

There are times when Mr. Dewey seems ready to admit this deficiency. In Reconstruction in Philosophy he was aware of the danger of utilitarian monsters, driving hard bargains with nature,

and he was appreciative, to a degree unusual in his thought, of the contemplative life, with its loving intercourse with forms and shapes and symbols in their immediacy. The weakness of Mr. Dewey's instrumentalism is a weakness of practical emphasis. He recognizes the place of the humane arts, but his preoccupation has been with science and technology, with instrumentalism in the narrow sense, the sense in which it occurs to Mr. Babbitt and to all his followers who practice so assiduously the mechanical ritual of American life. Conscious of the weakness of the academic critic, who may take art as an abstract end-in-itself, quite divorced from life and experience, he forgets that Mr. Babbitt treats showerbath fixtures and automobile gadgets in the same way — as if a life spent in the pursuit of these contrivances was a noble and liberal one. What Mr. Dewey has done in part has been to bolster up and confirm by philosophic statement tendencies which are already strong and well-established in American life, whereas he has been apathetic or diffident about things which must still be introduced into our scheme of things if it is to become thoroughly humane and significant. What I have said of William James applies with considerable force to his disciple.

In the revulsion that followed America's entry into the war, Randolph Bourne, one of Mr. Dewey's most ardent and talented disciples, found himself bereft of the philosophy which had once seemed all-sufficient; its counsel of adjustment left him rebelliously turning his back on the war-situation and the war-technique. In his recoil, Bourne put his finger upon the shallow side of Mr. Dewey's thinking; and his criticism is all the more adequate and pertinent because it rested on a sympathetic understanding of the instrumentalist philosophy.

"To those of us," he wrote, "who have taken Dewey's philosophy almost as our American religion, it never occurred that values could be subordinated to technique. We were instrumentalist, but we had our private utopias so clearly before our minds that the means fell always into place as contributory. And Dewey, of course, always meant his philosophy, when taken as a philosophy of life, to start with values. But there was always that unhappy ambiguity in his doctrine as to just how values were created, and it became easier and easier to assume that just any growth was justified and almost any activity valuable so long as it achieved its ends. The American, in living out his philosophy, has habitually confused results with product, and been content with getting somewhere without asking too closely whether it was the desirable place to get. . . . You must have your vision, and you must have your technique. The practical effect of Dewey's philosophy has evidently been to develop the sense of the latter at the expense of the former."

Without these superimposed values, the values that arise out of vision, instrumentalism becomes the mere apotheosis of actualities: it is all dressed up, with no place to go. Unfortunately, since the breakup of medieval culture, with such interludes as humanism and romanticism have supplied, men have subordinated the imagination to their interest in practical arrangements and expediences, or they have completely canalized the imagination itself into the practical channels of invention. This has led not alone to the conquest of the physical environment but also to the maceration of human purposes. The more men go on in this way, the farther they go from the domain of the imagination, and the more impossible it becomes for them to recognize the part that vision must play in bringing all their practical activities into a common focus. Their external determinism is only a reflection of their internal impotence: their "it must" can be translated "we can't." As Bourne said, the whole industrial world — and instrumentalism is only its highest conscious expression — has taken values for granted; and the result is that we are the victims of any chance set of values which happens to be left over from the past, or to become the fashion. We are living on fragments of the old cultures, or on abortions of the new, because the energies that should have gone into the imaginative life are balked at the source by the pervasive instrumentalism of the environment.

An instrumental philosophy which was oriented towards a whole life would begin, I think, not by a criticism of obsolete cultural values — which are already criticized by the fact that they are obsolete and inoperative and the possession of a small academic class — it would begin, rather, by a criticism of this one-sided idealization of practical contrivances. We shall not get much nearer a genuine culture by ignoring all the products of the creative imagination, or by palming off our practical instrumentalities — excellent though they are in their place — as their full equivalent. "If your ideal is to be adjustment to the situation," as Bourne well said, "in radiant coöperation with reality, then your success is likely to be just that, and no more. You never transcend anything. . . . Vision must constantly outshoot technique, opportunist efforts usually achieve even less than what obviously seemed possible. An impossibilist *élan* that appeals to desire will often carry farther. A philosophy of adjustment will not even make for adjustment."

Brave words! The pragmatists have been defeated, these last few centuries, because they have not searched for the kingdom, the power, and the glory together, but have sought to achieve power alone; so that the kingdom ceased to be a tangible one, and they knew no glory, except that which flowed out of their pursuit of power. Without vision, the pragmatists perish. And our generation, in particular, who have seen them fall back, one by one, into commercial affairs, into administrative absorption, into a pained abandonment of "reform," into taking whatever fortune thrusts into their laps, into an acquiescence even more pathetic, perhaps, than that of the disabled generation which followed the Civil War — our generation may well doubt the adequacy of their complaisant philosophy. "Things are in the saddle," Emerson said, "and ride mankind." We must overthrow the rider, before we can recover the horse: for otherwise, horse and rider may drive to the devil.

John Dewey: THE PRAGMATIC ACQUIESCENCE

THERE are myths and myths. Some are inspiriting; some are benumbing. Nature myths, at least in their first form, inspire because they are spontaneous responses of imagination to the scene that confronts it. Myths of literary criticism and historic interpretation are deadening. They do not enliven; they force subject-matter into ready-made patterns and thus dull sensitivity of perception. Such myths grow up in interpretations of past philosophies and always tend to overlay and conceal the realities of past reflection. They flourish in those literary versions by which the ideas of philosophers reach the public — for philosophers themselves are usually too much preoccupied with the technique, the professional rules, of their calling to have a public — except one another. Even such new movements as pragmatism and instrumentalism already have their accretion of myths which stand in place of the ideas themselves. Probably the unfortunate names themselves invite the creation and encourage the spread of these myths. The names account alike for some of the vogue of the doctrines and for some of the condemnation they receive.

One reading of the myth is embodied in the words which form the caption of what I am writing. They are borrowed from Lewis Mumford's The Golden Day; they sum up his essential criticism. "William James," he says, "gave this attitude of compromise and acquiescence a name: he called it pragmatism." Not content with this epithet, he headlines the idea of acquiescence; "the pragmatism that followed it was a paralysis." And again, "pragmatism was a blessed anaesthetic." What is denoted by "this attitude?" And in what did James acquiesce? The America of his own time, according to Mr.

Reprinted by permission from the *New Republic*, XLIX (January 5, 1927), 186–189.

Mumford, the America of the Gilded Age that followed the Civil War. More concerned with making clear his pattern than he is with William James he goes as far as to say, "James was only warming over again in philosophy the hash of everyday experience in the Gilded Age." And this of William James, the arch-heretic of his day, the intellectual non-conformist, the constant protester against everything institutionalized in action and belief, the valiant fighter for causes which if not lost were unpopular and conventionally ignored! Such are the exigencies and dangers of a myth. If one were to apply Mr. Mumford's method to his own treatment, one might regard him as the acquiescent prophet of the Slogan Age of the 1920's.

For some reason, Mr. Mumford is fairer to me than he is to William James. But to bring me into line with his formula he has to attribute to me ideas of democracy and of "adjustment" which I not only have never held, but against which I have consistently, if vainly, taught and written. As evidence of a willing surrender on my part to industrial utilitarianism, he cites the following passage from my writings: "Fine art, consciously undertaken as such, is peculiarly instrumental in quality. It is a device in experimentation carried on for the sake of education. It exists for the sake of a specialized use, use being a training of new modes of perception," etc. The reader of the passage would inevitably infer what Mr. Mumford intends him to infer, that the passage represents my view of fine art, namely, that it is merely instrumental in character. But the entire chapter from which it is extracted is a statement that all art which is really fine exhibits experience when it attains completion of a "final," consummatory character, and, while it is urged that such art is also contributory, that to

which it is held to be auxiliary is "renewal of spirit," not, it would seem, a base end, and certainly not a utilitarian one. The passage cited is directed against those views of fine art which treat it as an experience apart and for the few, an esoteric experience, instead of as a perfecting of the potentialities of any and all experience. This reference is implied in the quoted phrase "consciously undertaken as such"; it is explicitly stated in words which immediately precede what is cited, namely "seclusive aestheticians," the point being that fine art conceived in *their* sense is "instrumental," so that while all value is not denied to it, its value consists in opening "new objects to be observed and enjoyed." The next sentence after those which Mr. Mumford quotes, reads as follows: "This is a genuine service, but only an age of combined confusion and conceit will arrogate to works that perform this special utility the exclusive name of fine art." My literary style must indeed be "fuzzy and formless," as Mr. Mumford calls it, to have led him to assign to me a definition of fine art which I assert indicates combined confusion and conceit.

William James, however, hardly needs defense, certainly not against shaping him to a pattern which inverts his whole spirit and thought, and I do not think that a few more misconceptions of my own ideas are of such importance as to justify writing the present article. What has been said is introductory to an issue which is of genuine significance. What is the relation of criticism to the social life criticized? What, more particularly, is the relation of philosophy to its social medium and generation? I doubt if any competent student of the history of thought would say that there has existed any philosophy which amounted to anything which was merely a formulated acquiescence in the immediately pre-dominating traits of its day. Such things need no formulation, not even an apolo-getics; they dominate and that is enough for them. Yet there is probably also no historic philosophy which is not in some measure a reflection, an idealization, a justification of some of the tendencies of its own age. Yet what makes it a work of reflection and criticism is that the ele-ments and values selected are set in opposition to other factors, and those perhaps the ones most in evidence, the most clamorous, the most insistent; which is to say that all serious thinking com-bines in some proportion and perspective the actual and the possible, where actual-ity supplies contact and solidity while possibility furnishes the ideal upon which criticism rests and from which creative effort springs. The question whether the possibility appealed to is a possibility of the actual, or is externally imported and applied, is crucial.

There is a sense, then, in which prag-matic philosophy is a report of actual social life; in the same sense it is true of any philosophy that is not a private and quickly forgotten intellectual excres-cence. Not that philosophers set out to frame such reports. They are usually too much preoccupied with the special tradi-tions within which their work is done to permit the assumption of any such task. They are concerned with doing the best they can with problems and issues which come to them from the conflict of their professional traditions, which, therefore, are specialized and technical, and through which they see the affairs of the contem-porary scene only indirectly and, alas, darkly. Nevertheless, being human they may retain enough humanity to be, sub-consciously at least, sensitive to the nontechnical, nonprofessional, tendencies and issues of their own civilizations, and

to find in the peculiar characteristics of this civilization subjects for inquiry and analysis. In any case, it is as necessary as it is legitimate that their methods and results should, in their leading features, be translated out of their proper techni-cal context and set in a freer and more public landscape. The product of the dis-location may surprise no one more than the author of the technical doctrines. But without it the ulterior and significant meaning of the doctrines is neither liber-ated nor tested. The office of the literary and social critic in dealing with the broader human relationship of special-ized philosophical thinking is, accord-ingly, to be cherished. But the office is a difficult one to perform, more difficult to do well than that of technical philoso-phizing itself, just as any truly liberal human work is harder to achieve than is a technical task. Preconceptions, fixed patterns, too urgent desire to point a moral, are almost fatal. A pattern is im-plied in such critical interpretation, but it must be tridimensional and flowing, not linear and tight.

What, then, is to be said of pragmatism and of instrumentalism when they are viewed as reflective reports of the Ameri-can scene? More specifically, admitting a certain connection between the thought of James and the pioneer phase of Amer-ican life and between instrumentalism and our industrialism, how is that con-nection to be understood? Mr. Mumford recognizes that the reflection by James of pioneer life is genuine and significant as far as it goes. But, he says, a "valuable philosophy must take into account a greater range of experience than the dominating ones of a single generation." Doubtless: nevertheless the dominating tendencies of two or three centuries may reveal to a genial mind something of vast significance for all generations. Their

very exaggeration may disclose something hitherto concealed, while the lack
of that something may have introduced
such distortion and thinness into the
earlier intellectual picture that its dis-
closure operates as a transformation. Mr.
Mumford says that James lacked a *Welt-
Anschauung*. No sentence he could have
uttered affords such a measure of his
competency to state the relation which
the thought of James bore to pioneer-
dom. The idea of a universe which is not
all closed and settled, which is still in
some respects indeterminate and in the
making, which is adventurous and which
implicates all who share in it, whether by
acting or believing, in its own perils, may
appear to Mr. Mumford a commonplace,
and not to be reckoned as a *Welt-
Anschauung*. But one who has not
studied James patiently enough to learn
how this idea is wrought into his treatment of all special topics, from the will
to believe to his pluralism, from his radical empiricism to his moral and religious
ideas, has not got far in knowledge of
James. That the controlling *Welt-
Anschauung* does not appear in formal
and pompous logical parade in discussion of special topics may not make the
task of the would-be critic easy. But the
style shows how genuinely and spon-
taneously the leading idea pervades his
thinking. No other mode of literary presentation could have been so faithful to
the central thought.

Perhaps one has to be old enough to
recall, with some fullness of impression,
the intellectual atmosphere in which
James's work was carried on to realize
that James brought with him not only a
Welt-Anschauung but a revolutionary
one. His professional contemporaries did
not even trouble to criticize his philosophy; it was enough to laugh. Was it not
self-evidently a more or less delightful

whimsy of a tyro in philosophy who happened at the same time to be tempera-
mentally something of a genius in psychology? Not until he gathered together
the ideas which long previously he had
profusely scattered in his other writings
under the rather unfortunate title of
pragmatism did he receive serious attention. And long after "pragmatism" in any
sense save as an application of his *Welt-
Anschauung* shall have passed into a not
unhappy oblivion, the fundamental idea
of an open universe in which uncertainty,
choice, hypotheses, novelties and possibilities are naturalized will remain associated with the name of James; the more
he is studied in his historic setting the
more original and daring will the idea
appear. And if perchance the future historian associates the generation of the
idea with a pioneer America — in which
James had no personal share — that historian may be trusted to see that such an
idea is removed as far as pole from pole
from the temper of an age whose occu-
pation is acquisition, whose concern is
with security, and whose creed is that
the established economic régime is peculiarly "natural" and hence immutable in
principle.

But America is now industrial and
technological, not pioneering. Perhaps
the later form of pragmatism called instrumentalism is the anodyne to reconcile
the imagination and desire of man to the
brutalities and perversions of this aspect
of our life? Well, natural science and
the technology which has issued from it
are dominant tendencies of present culture, more conspicuously prominent in
the United States than elsewhere, but
everywhere all but universal in scope.
That preoccupation with them should,
whether consciously or subconsciously,
have played a part in generating "instrumentalism" is a not unreasonable hypoth-

esis. What then? If one confronts this phenomenon and does not withdraw for consolation to the "pillaging" of other climes and epochs, what is to be done with it? It needs criticism, not acquiescence: granted. But there is no criticism without understanding. And no matter how much one may draw upon contrasting phases of life, Greek, Indian with Mr. Santayana, or the Golden Day of Emerson, Thoreau, and Whitman with Mr. Mumford, for aid in this understanding, it is also true that without an understanding of natural science and technology in their own terms, understanding is external, arbitrary, and criticism is "transcendent" and ultimately of one's own private conceit.

Words, especially epithets, in philosophy are far from self-explaining. But the term "instrumentalism" might suggest to a mind not too precommitted, that natural science and technology are conceived as instruments, and that the logical intellect of mind which finds its congenial materials in these subjects is also instrumental — that is to say, not final, not complete, not the truth or reality of the world and life. Instruments imply, I should suppose, ends to which they are put, purposes that are not instruments which control them, values for which tools and agencies are to be used. The record of philosophy doubtless presents instances of almost utter self-contradiction and self-stultification. But it would require a mind unusually devoid both of sense of logic and a sense of humor — if there be any difference between them — to try to universalize instrumentalism, to set up a doctrine of tools which are not tools for anything except for more tools. The counterpart of "instrumentalism" is precisely that the values by which Mr. Mumford sets such store are the ends for the attainment of which natural science and all technologies and industries and industriousnesses are intrinsically, not externally and transcendentally, or by way of exhortation, contributory. The essential and immanent criticism of existing industrialism and of the dead weight of science is that instruments are made into ends, that they are deflected from their intrinsic quality and thereby corrupted. The implied idealization of science and technology is not by way of acquiescence. It is by way of appreciation that the ideal values which dignify and give meaning to human life have themselves in the past been precarious in possession, arbitrary, accidental and monopolized in distribution, because of lack of means of control; by lack, in other words, of those agencies and instrumentalities with which natural science through technologies equips mankind. Not all who say Ideals, Ideals, shall enter the kingdom of the ideal, but those who know and who respect the roads that conduct to the kingdom.

Louis Mumford:

THE PRAGMATIC ACQUIESCENCE: A Reply

SIR: In dealing with Mr. John Dewey's criticism of The Golden Day I have an ignoble advantage. I fired my shots in cold blood: he has retaliated in a mood that, alas! has spoiled his aim a little. Were it not for Mr. Dewey's position as a philosopher, I could afford to let his article speak for itself: but I respect his place and his claim too sincerely not to feel the duty of making a reply. In order to meet Mr. Dewey on the ground he has chosen, the reply shall take the form of a personal confession.

Let me first, however, make myself clear on one point. Mr. Dewey reproaches me with bringing him into line with a "formula," by deliberately misquoting and misunderstanding a passage at the end of Chapter Nine in his Experience and Nature. The paragraph in which Mr. Dewey brings this charge is not, precisely, a model of fair quotation; and lest any reader think that Mr. Dewey has scored off me here, I would only ask that he examine Mr. Dewey's chapter as a whole, and compare it with my criticism in The Golden Day, rather than in Mr. Dewey's report. I should be happy to think that Mr. Dewey and I agreed on what constitutes fine art. In the passage he refers to, his writing is a very elaborate barricade against such understanding and agreement.

This is the only issue Mr. Dewey has raised that concerns my morals as a critic. Let me now discuss the general issues.

Mr. Dewey is surprised and pained at the criticism of William James particularly because I have not followed the popular estimate nor accepted the usual stereotypes of "modern," "experimental," "radical" as eulogistic descriptions of their philosophies. I am honored that Mr. Dewey chose The Golden Day to stand the brunt of his attack: but where on earth has he been these last ten years, not to have felt the sting of this criticism before? Roughly speaking, most of my generation began as pragmatists. I studied Pragmatism and A Pluralistic Universe before I had read a word of Plato, and I knew something about "utilitarian idealism" many years before I had read Aristotle or Spinoza. Randolph Bourne was a professed follower of James and Dewey; and the very first biographic note appended to an article of mine in 1914 proudly stated that I was a pragmatist.

I do not renounce that early claim: I have learned much from Mr. Dewey and trust that I will learn more. But pragmatism as an approach to life must be judged by its own criterion; and as a complete philosophic orientation, it has come to seem to many of us, not false, but insufficient. I can claim no originality in arriving at this perception: Bourne reached it before me: so did Van Wyck Brooks in Letters and Leadership: so did Waldo Frank in Our America. We were, perhaps, the ungrateful heirs of William

Reprinted by permission from New Republic, XLIX (January 19, 1927), 250–251.

James's great liberation; but it was part of our sad experience to find that the philosophy which had rescued the academic world from an arid theological provincialism was in itself also a provincialism.

Mr. Dewey reiterates with praise William James's central intuition of a "universe which is not all closed and settled, which is still in some respects indeterminate and in the making, which is adventurous"— and so forth: but the fact is that Emerson had expressed all these things a whole generation before James. James's singular achievement was to articulate an academic skeleton, which in Emerson's writings had body and flesh. Now, in no place have I belittled this contribution of James, derivative though it was. I specifically said that "the feeling of boundless possibility that springs from James's pages was one of the healthy influences of the frontier." But however thoroughly this feeling infused itself, with all its implications, in James's philosophy and gave it its twist of novelty and originality, it scarcely sufficed as a complete Anschauung. The fact that William James's philosophy could seem to upset the academic universe only shows in what a small universe his contemporaries dwelt.

What was the most important consequence of Pragmatism? One of the most important, surely, was Mr. Dewey; for he carried the Jamesian outlook into the industrial world. In The Golden Day I said that "the weakness of Mr. Dewey's instrumentalism is a weakness of practical emphasis. He recognizes the place of the humane arts, but his preoccupation has been with science and technology, with instrumentalism in the narrow sense, the sense in which it occurs to Mr. Babbitt and to all his followers who practice so assiduously the mechanical ritual of

American life." In his present defense, Mr. Dewey has, unfortunately, exhibited his confusion and his bias once again. Living in a world which, for lack of other interests and diversions, has directed all its energies into the mechanical arts and the knowledge that makes them possible, he talks as if the means necessary to the fulfillment of ends or ideals were inevitably scientific or mechanical means. Hence his belief that simply by understanding science and technology conceived as instruments we are in a better position to fulfill the ends of life itself.

This is one of the theological dogmas of the industrial age; and one has only to translate it into concrete terms to see that it is nonsense. The people who originally built and worshiped in Chartres appreciated fine art, if any community ever did; their appreciation was not the exclusive possession of a leisure class. Did they need lithography, illustrated lectures and historic guidebooks to achieve the spiritual state in which fine art became a function of their daily life? If they did, or if our own position in the fine arts is superior, Mr. Dewey is right. If they didn't, then science and technology have a limited and not a universal function in describing and modifying the world we live in.

The point is that the sum total of life has a much greater sphere than that which science, technology, or its philosophic counterpart, instrumentalism, habitually covers. Feeling this lack in the body of Mr. Dewey's thought, if not in its abstract outline, our generation has reached out to other thinkers and has attempted to assimilate to its own experience the elements that physical science and technology squeezed out of the foreground. Spinoza, Santayana, Croce, or in my particular case, Plato and Patrick

Geddes, have given us a hold on wider realms of thought and life than the pragmatists have been interested in. This does not mean that we have lost contact with the industrial world, or retreated from it. Speaking merely for myself, the interest in technology, which made me enter a technical high school at thirteen, become a laboratory helper in the Bureau of Standards, and a professional radio operator has persisted: it forms a basis for my active interests in architecture, city planning and regional development.

At every turn in dealing with this practical world, however, we are faced by the fact that knowledge of the necessary technique is common enough to be taken for granted, and that the ability to conceive new forms and channels for life to run in, the ability to think creatively with the artist who says "I will" rather than causally with the scientist who says "It must" is what is lacking. The desiccation and sterilization of the imaginative life has been quite as important an historic fact as the growth of a sense of causality, an insight into what Mr. Dewey calls "means-consequences." Acting alone, without a counterpoise in the creative imagination, our narrow instrumentalism has left us impotent: all the "agencies and instrumentalities with which natural science through technologies equips mankind" will not in this situation help us much more than the king's horses and men helped Humpty-Dumpty.

Mr. Dewey seems to believe that the "ends" or "ideals" will come into existence of themselves, if only we pay careful heed to the means. I do not share this belief, and in view of what has happened during the last three centuries, it seems to me one of bland complaisance or blind optimism. A world that has cheerfully accepted Mr. Dewey's attitude

is neither puzzled nor horrified by the fact that a great line of creative artists in literature and painting have been maimed or rebellious men. If I have allied myself, more by instinct than by intention, with architects, it is because they have the professional distinction of thinking both scientifically, in terms of means, and imaginatively, in terms of the humanly desirable ends for which these means exist.

Does this make a little clearer the source of the breach that exists between Mr. Dewey and a whole group of the relatively younger critics? It is not that we reject Mr. Dewey: that would be ingratitude: but that we seek for a broader field and a less provincial interpretation of Life and Nature than he has given us. Far from trying to fit the facts of The Golden Day to a pre-ordained pattern, I did Mr. Dewey the historic justice of separating him from James, and of giving him credit for participating in the active but bewildered idealism of the last twenty years — a more vigorous and realistic period, in many ways, than that which followed the Civil War. If there is malice in the treatment, the facts are responsible: Mr. Santayana might quite as well reproach me for his being placed beside Mrs. Jack Gardner. That Mr. Dewey elbowed Mr. Dreiser, figuratively speaking, in Chicago, and unconsciously absorbed a somewhat similar point of view and similar literary habit is a matter of history; the virtue of the historic method is that understanding leads to pardon!

In The Golden Day I have hinted that there are two Deweys, the central Dewey of the formative period, and another Dewey, still thinking experimentally and freshly, who is reaching out to wider sources of experience. The latter Dewey is the philosopher who has embraced certain aspects of modern art and who hailed Whitehead's *Science and The Modern World* as a change in the intellectual climate. Did I have the misfortune to rouse the older Dewey into a position of defense, rather than put the new one in a mood of courteous inquisition? If the fault has been mine, I apologize; if it is remediable, I will make amends.

John Dewey: PRAGMATIC AMERICA

IN a recent number of the *Freeman* Bertrand Russell writes: "The two qualities which I consider superlatively important are love of truth and love of our neighbor. I find love of truth in America obscured by commercialism of which pragmatism is the philosophical expression; and love of our neighbor kept in fetters by Puritan morality." The statement comes to us with double importance. For it is obviously dictated by Mr. Russell's own love of truth and love for us as his neighbor. Police records and newspaper columns do not seem to indicate that Puritanism is effective in fettering our love for our neighbor's wife however much it restricts our love for him. If pragmatism is the intellectual reflection of commercialism, pragmatists seem to be assured of a speedy victory of their philosophy in England and the continent of Europe; for there are rumors, apparently authentic, that commercialism exists in strength in these outlying parts of the world. But such matters may be passed over, especially as Mr. Russell tells us that he is aware that the evils he finds in us are not unknown in the rest of the world, and that he urges their potency among us because we are more complacent, more boastful of our "idealism," less possessed of a critical minority than is the old world.

Mr. Russell is probably not entirely alone in the world in regarding love of truth and of neighbor as the two supreme human excellences. In the United States there are those who agree, at least in profession. The fact that the belief had some currency before he voiced it makes it the more important to consider the state of these virtues, and the power of their enemies among us. One otherwise attractive line of discussion is closed to us. We cannot cite evidence that we compare favorably with the rest of humanity in love of truth, and possibly a little more than favorably in respect to love of neighbors. For such a method turns against us. It is just another sample of our obdurate complacency, of the rationalizing idealization with which we obscure our critical perception of the truth.

The suggestion that pragmatism is the intellectual equivalent of commercialism need not, however, be taken too seriously. It is of that order of interpretation which would say that English neo-realism is a reflection of the aristocratic snobbery of the English; the tendency of

Reprinted by permission from *New Republic*, XXX (April 12, 1922), 185–187.

French thought to dualism an expression of an alleged Gallic disposition to keep a mistress in addition to a wife; and the idealism of Germany a manifestation of an ability to elevate beer and sausage into a higher synthesis with the spiritual values of Beethoven and Wagner. Nor does the figure of William James exist in exact correspondence with a glorification of commercialism. The man who wrote that "callousness to abstract justice is *the* sinister feature of United States civilization," that this callousness is a "symptom of the moral flabbiness born of the exclusive worship of the bitch-goddess SUCCESS," and that this worship "together with the squalid cash interpretation put upon the word success is our national disease" was not consciously nor unconsciously engaged in an intellectual formulation of the spirit he abhorred. Nor was Charles Peirce conspicuous for conformity to commercial standards. Emotional irritation coexists in our humanity with the consideration that love of truth is a superlative good, and it is capable upon occasion of blinding that love.

Nevertheless, there is something instructive about our spiritual estate in the fact that pragmatism was born upon American soil, and that pragmatism presents consequences as a test and a responsibility of the life of reason. Historically the fact is testimony to "Anglo-Saxon" kinship; it is testimony to spiritual kinship with Bacon, who wrote that "truth and utility are the very same thing, and works themselves are of greater value as pledges of truth than as contributing to the comforts of life"; who taught that the end and the test of science and philosophy are their fruits for the relief and betterment of the estate of humanity; while also holding that converting science and philosophy to immediate fruitage for lucre and reputation is

their curse. American pragmatism is testimony that the tradition of Bacon carried on in divers ways by Hobbes, Locke and Hume has taken root here.

Yet there is special significance in the fact that this tradition was first revived and then made central by Peirce and James in the United States. Anyone who wishes to take a census of our spiritual estate (along with the censorship implied in a census) will assuredly find the pragmatic spirit important. It is a commonplace, however, that strength and weakness, excellence and defect, go together, because they are the two sides of the same thing. If, therefore, love of truth is to express itself in a discriminating way, it must be willing to attach itself to our sense that consequences are the test and the token of responsibility in the operation of intelligence until its significance is extracted. It is not in the first instance a question of the truth of this feeling. The disposition may be, if you please, as obnoxious to ultimate philosophic truth as it is repellent to certain temperaments. But first we have to find out what it means, what it means for both good and bad. Love of truth is manifest in desire to understand rather than in hurry to praise and blame.

A conviction that consequences in human welfare are a test of the worth of beliefs and thoughts has some obvious beneficial aspects. It makes for a fusion of the two superlatively important qualities, love of truth and love of neighbor. It discourages dogmatism and its child, intolerance. It arouses and heartens an experimental spirit which wants to know how systems and theories work before giving complete adhesion. It militates against too sweeping and easy generalizations, even against those which would indict a nation. Compelling attention to details, to particulars, it safeguards one from seclusion in universals; one is obliged, as William James was always saying, to get down from noble aloofness into the muddy stream of concrete things. It fosters a sense of the worth of communication of what is known. This takes effect not only in education, but in a belief that we do not fully know the meaning of anything till it has been imparted, shared, made common property. I well remember the remark of an unschooled American pioneer, who said of a certain matter that some day it would not only be found out, but it would be known. He was ignorant of books, but he declared the profound philosophy that nothing is really known till it operates in the common life.

Any such attitude is clearly a faith, not a demonstration. It too can be demonstrated only in *its* works, its fruits. Therefore it is not a facile thing. It commits us to a supremely difficult task. Perhaps the task is too hard for human nature. The faith may demonstrate its own falsity by failure. We may be arrested on the plane of commercial "success"; we may be diverted to search for consequences easier to achieve, and may noisily acclaim superficial and even disastrous "works" and fruits as proof of genuine success instead of evidence of failure. We not only may do so, but we actually are doing so. If the course of history be run, if our present estate be final, no honest soul can claim that success exceeds failure. Perhaps this will always remain the case. Humanity is not conspicuous for having made a successful job of life anywhere. But an honest soul will also admit that the failure is not due to inherent defects in the faith, but to the fact that its demands are too high for human power; that mankind is not up to making good the requirements of the faith, or at least that that part of a common humanity which inhabits these United States is not up to it, and that the experiment

must be passed on to another place and time.

Yet the gloomiest view reminds us of another phase of the pragmatic faith. Undoubtedly in expressing his sense of a world still open, a world still in the making, William James reported, perhaps with some superfluous accretions of romanticism to his native idiom, a characteristic feature of the American scene. Be the evils what they may, the experiment is not yet played out. The United States are not yet made; they are not a finished fact to be categorically assessed. Mr. James' assertion that the world is still making does not import a facile faith. He knew well that the world has also its madeness, and that what is done and over with fearfully complicates the task of making the future that human better we should like it to be.

A discriminating spiritual census of the United States will, therefore, ask about the already made things which we inherit and which mix with our creative making to arrest, divert and pervert it. After all we inherit from a Europe which was, compared with our scene, a made affair. Every day our cities are eloquent of the past fruits of a feudal Europe. His power far exceeds mine who can tell just how much of our present ill is due to the commercialism which is of our making and how much is due to deposit of an ancient feudalism. Commerce itself, let us dare to say it, is a noble thing. It is intercourse, exchange, communication, distribution, sharing of what is otherwise secluded and private. Commercialism like all isms is evil. That we have not as yet released commerce from bondage to private interests is proof of the solidity and tenacity of our European heritage. Commerce in knowledge, in intelligence, is still a side-issue, precarious, spasmodic, corrupt. Pragmatic faith walks in chains, not erect.

One other heritage of things already made still has to be reckoned with, reckoned with in social practice as well as in formulation. These United States were born when the pragmatic and experimental faith of the English tradition was in eclipse. Bacon did not exaggerate the control of nature to be obtained from study of nature. But he enormously underestimated that inertia of social forces which would resist free application of the new power to the relief and betterment of the human estate, and which would effect a private monopolization of the fruits of the new power of knowledge. Those who were called liberals lost their faith in experimental method. They were seduced into desiring a creed as absolute, as final, as eternal as that wielded by their opponents. The dogma of natural rights of the individual was the product. The pioneer, agrarian American scene was a congenial home for the new dogma. We tied ourselves down to political and legal practices and institutions radically hostile to our native disposition and endeavor. Legalism, along with feudalized commercialism, is wedded to commercialism, is the anti-pragmatic "made" which hinders and perverts our pragmatic makings. It is incarnate in constitutions and courts. The resulting situation is not one which calls for complacency. But the beginning of improvement is to place responsibility where it belongs.

Our noisy and nauseating "idealism" is an expression of the emotions which would cover and disguise a mixed situation. There is a genuine idealism of faith in the future, in experiment directed by intelligence, in the communication of knowledge, in the rights of the common man to a common share in the fruits of the spirit. This spirit when it works does not need to talk. But its workings are paralyzed here, arrested there, and more or less corrupted everywhere by a feudalized commercialism and a legalism which we cover up with eloquent speeches because we do not honestly confront them. Discrimination is the first fruit of love of truth and of love of neighbor. Till we discriminate we shall oscillate between wholesale revulsion and the sloppy idealism of popular emotion.

Reinhold Niebuhr:
MORAL MAN AND IMMORAL SOCIETY

THE thesis to be elaborated in these pages is that a sharp distinction must be drawn between the moral and social behavior of individuals and of social groups, national, racial, and economic; and that this distinction justifies and necessitates political policies which a purely individualistic ethic must always find embarrassing. The title "Moral Man and Immoral Society" suggests the intended distinction too unqualifiedly, but it is nevertheless a fair indication of the

Reprinted from *Moral Man and Immoral Society* by Reinhold Niebuhr; copyright 1932 by Charles Scribner's Sons; used by permission of the publishers.

argument to which the following pages are devoted. Individual men may be moral in the sense that they are able to consider interests other than their own in determining problems of conduct, and are capable, on occasion, of preferring the advantages of others to their own. They are endowed by nature with a measure of sympathy and consideration for their kind, the breadth of which may be extended by an astute social pedagogy. Their rational faculty prompts them to a sense of justice which educational discipline may refine and purge of egoistic elements until they are able to view a social situation, in which their own interests are involved, with a fair measure of objectivity. But all these achievements are more difficult, if not impossible, for human societies and social groups. In every human group there is less reason to guide and to check impulse, less capacity for self-transcendence, less ability to comprehend the needs of others and therefore more unrestrained egoism than the individuals, who compose the group, reveal in their personal relationships.

The inferiority of the morality of groups to that of individuals is due in part to the difficulty of establishing a rational social force which is powerful enough to cope with the natural impulses by which society achieves its cohesion; but in part it is merely the revelation of a collective egoism, compounded of the egoistic impulses of individuals, which achieve a more vivid expression and a more cumulative effect when they are united in a common impulse than when they express themselves separately and discreetly.

Inasfar as this treatise has a polemic interest it is directed against the moralists, both religious and secular, who imagine that the egoism of individuals is being progressively checked by the development of rationality or the growth of a religiously inspired good will and that nothing but the continuance of this process is necessary to establish social harmony between all the human societies and collectives. Social analyses and prophecies made by moralists, sociologists and educators upon the basis of these assumptions lead to a very considerable moral and political confusion in our day. They completely disregard the political necessities in the struggle for justice in human society by failing to recognise those elements in man's collective behavior which belong to the order of nature and can never be brought completely under the dominion of reason or conscience. They do not recognise that when collective power, whether in the form of imperialism or class domination, exploits weakness, it can never be dislodged unless power is raised against it. If conscience and reason can be insinuated into the resulting struggle they can only qualify but not abolish it.

The most persistent error of modern educators and moralists is the assumption that our social difficulties are due to the failure of the social sciences to keep pace with the physical sciences which have created our technological civilisation. The invariable implication of this assumption is that, with a little more time, a little more adequate moral and social pedagogy and a generally higher development of human intelligence, our social problems will approach solution. "It is," declares Professor John Dewey, "our human intelligence and our human courage which is on trial; it is incredible that men who have brought the technique of physical discovery, invention and use to such a pitch of perfection will abdicate in the face of the infinitely more important human problem. What stands in the way (of a planned economy) is a lot of outworn traditions, moth-eaten slogans and catchwords that do substitute duty for thought, as well as our entrenched predatory self-interest. We shall only make a real beginning in intelligent thought when we cease mouthing platitudes. . . . Just as soon as we begin to use the knowledge and skills we have, to control social consequences in the interest of a shared, abundant and secured life, we shall cease to complain of the backwardness of our social knowledge. . . . We shall then take the road which leads to the assured building up of social science just as men built up physical science when they actively used techniques and tools and numbers in physical experimentation."[1] In spite of Professor Dewey's great interest in and understanding of the modern social problem there is very little clarity in this statement. The real cause of social inertia, "our predatory self-interest," is mentioned only in passing without influencing his reasoning, and with no indication that he understands how much social conservatism is due to the economic interests of the owning classes. On the whole, social conservatism is ascribed to ignorance, a viewpoint which states only part of the truth and reveals the natural bias of the educator. The suggestion that we will only make a beginning in intelligent thought when we "cease mouthing platitudes," is itself so platitudinous that it rather betrays the confusion of an analyst who has no clear counsels about the way to overcome social inertia. The idea that we cannot be socially intelligent until we begin experimentation in social problems in the way that the physical scientists experimented fails to take account of an important difference between the physical and the social sciences. The physical sciences gained their freedom when they overcame the traditionalism based on ignorance, but the traditionalism which the social sciences face is based upon the economic interest of the dominant social classes who are trying to maintain their special privileges in society. Nor can the difference between the very character of social and physical sciences be overlooked. Complete rational objectivity in a social situation is impossible. The very social scientists who are so anxious to offer our generation counsels of salvation and are disappointed that an ignorant and slothful people are so slow to accept their wisdom, betray middle-class prejudices in almost everything they write. Since reason is always, to some degree, the servant of interest in a social situation, social injustice cannot be resolved by moral and rational suasion alone, as the educator and social scientist usually believes. Conflict is inevitable, and in this conflict power must be challenged by power. That fact is not recognized by most of the educators, and only very grudgingly admitted by most of the social scientists.

If social conflict be a part of the process of gaining social justice, the idea of most of Professor Dewey's disciples that our salvation depends upon the development of "experimental procedures"[2] in social life, commensurate with the experimentalism of the physical sciences, does not have quite the plausibility which they attribute to it. Contending factions in a social struggle require morale; and morale is created by the right dogmas, symbols and emotionally potent oversimplifications. These are at least as necessary as the scientific spirit of tentativity. No class of industrial

1 John Dewey, *Philosophy and Civilization* (New York: Minton, Balch), p. 329.

2 *Cf. inter alia*, John Childs, *Education and the Philosophy of Experimentalism*, p. 37.

workers will ever win freedom from the dominant classes if they give themselves completely to the "experimental techniques" of the modern educators. They will have to believe rather more firmly in the justice and in the probable triumph of their cause, than any impartial science would give them the right to believe, if they are to have enough energy to contest the power of the strong. They may be very scientific in projecting their social goal and in choosing the most effective instruments for its attainment, but a motive force will be required to nerve them for their task which is not easily derived from the cool objectivity of science. Modern educators are, like rationalists of all the ages, too enamored of the function of reason in life. The world of history, particularly in man's collective behavior, will never be conquered by reason, unless reason uses tools, and is itself driven by forces which are not rational.

The sociologists, as a class, understand the modern social problem even less than the educators. They usually interpret social conflict as the result of a clash between different kinds of "behavior patterns," which can be eliminated if the contending parties will only allow the social scientist to furnish them with a new and more perfect pattern which will do justice to the needs of both parties. With the educators they regard ignorance rather than self-interest as the cause of conflict. "Apparently," declares Kimball Young, "the only way in which collective conflicts, as well as individual conflicts, can be successfully and hygienically solved is by securing a redirection of behavior toward a more feasible environmental objective. This can be accomplished most successfully by the rational reconditioning of attitudes on a higher neuro-psychic or intellectual symbolic plane to the facts of science, preferably through a free discussion with a minimum of propaganda. This is not an easy road to mental and social sanity but it appears to be the only one which arrives at the goal."[3] Here a technique which works very well in individual relations, and in certain types of social conflict due to differences in culture, is made a general panacea. How is it to solve the problem between England and India? Through the Round-Table Conference? But how much would England have granted India at the conference if a non-co-operation campaign, a type of conflict, had not forced the issue?

A favorite counsel of the social scientists is that of accommodation. If two parties are in a conflict, let them, by conferring together, moderate their demands and arrive at a *modus vivendi*. This is, among others, the advice of Professor Hornell Hart.[4] Undoubtedly there are innumerable conflicts which must be resolved in this fashion. But will a disinherited group, such as the Negroes for instance, ever win full justice in society in this fashion? Will not even its most minimum demands seem exorbitant to the dominant whites, among whom only a very small minority will regard the inter-racial problem from the perspective of objective justice? Or how are the industrial workers to follow Professor Hart's advice in dealing with industrial owners, when the owners possess so much power that they can win the debate with the workers, no matter how unconvincing their arguments? Only a very few sociologists seem to have learned that an adjustment of a social conflict, caused by the disproportion of power in society, will hardly result in

[3] Kimball Young, *Social Attitudes*, p. 72.

[4] Hornell Hart, *The Science of Social Relations.*

justice as long as the disproportion of power remains. Sometimes the sociologists are so completely oblivious to the real facts of an industrial civilisation that, as Floyd Allport for instance, they can suggest that the unrest of industrial workers is due not to economic injustice but to a sense of inferiority which will be overcome just as soon as benevolent social psychologists are able to teach the workers that "no one is charging them with inferiority except themselves."[5] These omniscient social scientists will also teach the owners that "interests and profits must be tempered by regard for the worker." Thus "the socialisation of individual control" in industry will obviate the necessity of "socialistic control." Most of the social scientists are such unqualified rationalists that they seem to imagine that men of power will immediately check their exactions and pretensions in society, as soon as they have been apprised by the social scientists that their actions and attitudes are anti-social. Professor Clarence Marsh Case, in an excellent analysis of the social problem, places his confidence in a "reorganisation of values" in which, among other things, industrial leaders must be made to see "that despotically controlled industry in a society that professes democracy as an article of faith is an anachronism that cannot endure."[6] It may be that despotism cannot endure but it will not abdicate merely because the despots have discovered it to be anachronistic. Sir Arthur Salter, to name a brilliant economist among the social scientists, finishes his penetrating analysis of the distempers of our civilisation by expressing the usual hope that a higher intelligence or a sincerer morality will prevent the govern-

ments of the future from perpetrating the mistakes of the past. His own analysis proves conclusively that the failure of governments is due to the pressure of economic interest upon them rather than to the "limited capacities of human wisdom." In his own words "government is failing above all because it has become enmeshed in the task of giving discretionary, particularly preferential, privileges to competitive industry."[7] In spite of this analysis Sir Arthur expects the governments to redeem our civilisation by becoming more socially minded and he thinks that one method which will help them to do so is to "draw into the service of the public the great private institutions which represent the organised activities of the country, chambers of commerce, banking institutions, industrial and labor organisations." His entire hope for recovery rests upon the possibility of developing a degree of economic disinterestedness among men of power which the entire history of mankind proves them incapable of acquiring. It is rather discouraging to find such naïve confidence in the moral capacities of collective man, among men who make it their business to study collective human behavior. Even when, as Professor Howard Odum, they are prepared to admit that "conflict will be necessary" as long as "unfairness in the distribution of the rewards of labor exists," they put their hope in the future. They regard social conflict as only an expedient of the moment "until broader principles of education and cooperation can be established."[8] Anarchism, with an uncoerced and voluntary justice, seems to be either an explicit or implicit social goal of every second social scientist.

[5] Floyd Allport, *Social Psychology*, pp. 14–27.

[6] Clarence Marsh Case, *Social Process and Human Progress*, p. 233.

[7] Sir Arthur Salter, *Recovery*, p. 341.

[8] Howard W. Odum, *Man's Quest for Social Guidance*, p. 477.

Modern religious idealists usually follow in the wake of social scientists in advocating compromise and accommodation as the way to social justice. Many leaders of the church like to insist that it is not their business to champion the cause of either labor or capital, but only to admonish both sides to a spirit of fairness and accommodation. "Between the far-visioned capitalism of Owen Young and the hard-headed socialism of Ramsay MacDonald," declares Doctor Justin Wroe Nixon, "there is probably no impassable gulf. The progress of mankind . . . depends upon following the MacDonalds and Youngs into those areas."[9] Unfortunately, since those lines were written the socialism of MacDonald has been revealed as not particularly hard-headed, and the depression has shown how little difference there really is between Mr. Young's "new capitalism" and the older and less suave types of capitalism.

What is lacking among all these moralists, whether religious or rational, is an understanding of the brutal character of the behavior of all human collectives, and the power of self-interest and collective egoism in all intergroup relations. Failure to recognise the stubborn resistance of group egoism to all moral and inclusive social objectives inevitably involves them in unrealistic and confused political thought. They regard social conflict either as an impossible method of achieving morally approved ends or as a momentary expedient which a more perfect education or a purer religion will make unnecessary. They do not see that the limitations of the human imagination, the easy subservience of reason to prejudice and passion, and the consequent persistence of irrational egoism, particularly in group behavior, make social conflict an inevitability in human history, probably to its very end.

The romantic overestimate of human virtue and moral capacity, current in our modern middle-class culture, does not always result in an unrealistic appraisal of present social facts. Contemporary social situations are frequently appraised quite realistically, but the hope is expressed that a new pedagogy or a revival of religion will make conflict unnecessary in the future. Nevertheless a considerable portion of middle-class culture remains quite unrealistic in its analysis of the contemporary situation. It assumes that evidences of a growing brotherliness between classes and nations are apparent in the present moment. It gives such arrangements as the League of Nations, such ventures as the Kellogg Pact and such schemes as company industrial unions, a connotation of moral and social achievement which the total facts completely belie. "There must," declares Professor George Stratton, a social psychologist, "always be a continuing and widening progress. But our present time seems to promise distinctly the close of an old epoch in world relations and the opening of a new. . . . Under the solemn teaching of the War, most of the nations have made political commitments which are of signal promise for international discipline and for still further and more effective governmental acts."[10] This glorification of the League of Nations as a symbol of a new epoch in international relations has been very general, and frequently very unqualified, in the Christian churches, where liberal Christianity has given itself to the illusion that all social relations are being brought progressively under "the law of Christ." William

[9] Justin Wroe Nixon, *An Emerging Christian Faith*, p. 294.

[10] George M. Stratton, *Social Psychology and International Conduct*, pp. 355–361.

Adams Brown speaks for the whole liberal Christian viewpoint when he declares: "From many different centres and in many different forms the crusade for a unified and brotherly society is being carried on. The ideal of the League of Nations in which all civilised people shall be represented and in which they shall cooperate with one another in fighting common enemies like war and disease is winning recognition in circles which have hitherto been little suspected of idealism. . . . In relations between races, in strife between capital and labor, in our attitudes toward the weaker and more dependent members of society we are developing a social conscience, and situations which would have been accepted a generation ago as a matter of course are felt as an intolerable scandal."[11] Another theologian and pastor, Justin Wroe Nixon, thinks that "another reason for believing in the growth of social statesmanship on the part of business leaders is based upon their experience as trustees in various philanthropic and educational enterprises."[12] This judgment reveals the moral confusion of liberal Christianity with perfect clarity. Teachers of morals who do not see the difference between the problem of charity within the limits of an accepted social system and the problem of justice between economic groups, holding uneven power within modern industrial society, have simply not faced the most obvious differences between the morals of groups and those of individuals. The suggestion that the fight against disease is in the same category with the fight against war reveals the same confusion. Our contem-

porary culture fails to realise the power, extent and persistence of group egoism in human relations. It may be possible, though it is never easy, to establish just relations between individuals within a group purely by moral and rational suasion and accommodation. In inter-group relations this is practically an impossibility. The relations between groups must therefore always be predominantly political rather than ethical, that is, they will be determined by the proportion of power which each group possesses at least as much as by any rational and moral appraisal of the comparative needs and claims of each group. The coercive factors, in distinction to the more purely moral and rational factors, in political relations can never be sharply differentiated and defined. It is not possible to estimate exactly how much a party to a social conflict is influenced by a rational argument or by the threat of force. It is impossible, for instance, to know what proportion of a privileged class accepts higher inheritance taxes because it believes that such taxes are good social policy and what proportion submits merely because the power of the state supports the taxation policy. Since political conflict, at least in times when controversies have not reached the point of crisis, is carried on by the threat, rather than the actual use, of force, it is always easy for the casual or superficial observer to overestimate the moral and rational factors, and to remain oblivious to the covert types of coercion and force which are used in the conflict.

Whatever increase in social intelligence and moral goodwill may be achieved in human history, may serve to mitigate the brutalities of social conflict, but they cannot abolish the conflict itself. That could be accomplished only if human groups, whether racial, national or

11 William Adams Brown, *Pathways to Certainty*, p. 246.

12 Justin Wroe Nixon, *An Emerging Christian Faith*, p. 291.

economic, could achieve a degree of reason and sympathy which would permit them to see and to understand the interests of others as vividly as they understand their own, and a moral goodwill which would prompt them to affirm the rights of others as vigorously as they affirm their own. Given the inevitable limitations of human nature and the limits of the human imagination and intelligence, this is an ideal which individuals may approximate but which is beyond the capacities of human societies. Educators who emphasise the pliability

of human nature, social and psychological scientists who dream of "socialising" man and religious idealists who strive to increase the sense of moral responsibility, can serve a very useful function in society in humanising individuals within an established social system and in purging the relations of individuals of as much egoism as possible. In dealing with the problems and necessities of radical social change they are almost invariably confusing in their counsels because they are not conscious of the limitations in human nature whcih finally frustrate their efforts.

Mortimer J. Adler: GOD AND THE PROFESSORS

THE Founding Members of this Conference are, for the most part, professors in American colleges and universities. They are eminent representatives of the various academic disciplines, among which are the three mentioned as most relevant to this Conference — science, philosophy, and religion. The presence of historians and humanistic scholars is justified by the modern extension of science to include the so-called social sciences, with which all research about human affairs and culture can be affiliated. Most of these professors belong to one or more of the several learned societies which meet annually for the reading and discussion of papers that purport to make contributions to truth, or at least to what is academically recognized as learn-

ing. Hence, the reason for this Conference, for this additional meeting at which more papers are being read and discussed, must be some need for the professors to get together in a different way and for a different purpose. If the public wonders why we are gathering here this September, we must justify this Conference as trying to do something which is not, and perhaps cannot be, accomplished in the ordinary processes of our academic life — in classrooms, faculty meetings, or the sessions of learned societies.

Some explanations have already been given. We have come together because we all share, for different reasons and in varying degrees, an uneasiness about something we call the present situation.

From *Science, Philosophy and Religion: A Symposium* (New York: Conference on Science, Philosophy and Religion in Their Relation to the Democratic Way of Life, Inc., 1941). Reprinted by permission. [During September 10–11, 1940, a national Conference on Science, Philosophy and Religion in their relation to the Democratic Way of Life was held at the Jewish Theological Seminary, New York City. At the session devoted to philosophy, Mortimer J. Adler of the University of Chicago read this paper, which was widely reported and extensively cited in the press. Ed.]

Whether or not we are ready to say that God's in his heaven, we cry with one voice that all's not right with the world. I wish I could credit my colleagues with one further agreement, namely, that the present crisis is only superficially a conflict between democracy and totalitarianism in the political arena, or between individualism and collectivism in the economic sphere. If that were the full nature of the crisis, why should we waste time talking about science, philosophy and religion? The fact that we have chosen to consider three major components of human culture should indicate that we all have a vague sense of cultural disorder as the root of our troubles, as the source of a threatening doom. Far from being prime movers, Hitler and Mussolini, or, if you wish, the Stalins and Chamberlains, are but paranoiac puppets, dancing for a moment on the crest of the wave — the wave that is the historic motion of modern culture of its own destruction. A culture is not killed by political conflicts, even when they attain the shattering violence of modern warfare; nor by economic revolutions, even when they involve the dislocations of modern mass uprisings. A culture dies of diseases which are themselves cultural. It may be born sick, as modern culture was, or it may decay through insufficient vitality to overcome the disruptive forces present in every culture; but, in any case, cultural disorder is a cause and not an effect of the political and economic disturbances which beset the world today.

The health of a culture, like the health of the body, consists in the harmonious functioning of its parts. Science, philosophy and religion are certainly major parts of European culture; their distinction from one another as quite separate parts is certainly the most characteristic cultural achievement of modern times. But if they have not been properly distin-

guished, they cannot be properly related; and unless they are properly related, properly ordered to one another, cultural disorder, such as that of modern times, inevitably results. This Conference, one might suppose, has been called to consider the illness of our culture; more than that, to seek and effect remedies. One of the troubles is that scientists, philosophers, and theologians, or teachers of religion, have long failed to communicate with one another. The structure of a modern university, with its departmental separations, and its total lack of order among specialized disciplines, represents perfectly the disunity and chaos of modern culture. Since nothing can be expected of the professors locked up in their departmental cells, since reforming our institutions of higher learning (to make them truly universities) seems to be impossible, since the ordinary processes of academic life manifest the very defects which must be remedied, the professors have been assembled under the special auspices of this Conference with the hope that lines of communication can be established. That done, one might even hope for communication to lead to mutual understanding, and thence to agreement about the truths which could unify our culture.

If what I have said is not the purpose of this Conference, I can see no justification for it whatsoever. The fact that all the professors gathered mention the Present Crisis, without trying to agree about its nature and causes; the fact that they manifest some concern about Democracy, without trying to define it and understand its roots; the fact that, in a baffling variety of senses, they refer to Science, Philosophy and Religion, without trying to solve the intricate problem of the relationship of these disciplines, — all this amounts to nothing. An undertaking of this sort is not needed to make professors think or talk this way. Nor is it needed to give them an opportunity to write and read papers which do credit to their specialized scholarly achievements. Unless this be a Conference in more than name only, unless it be a concerted effort to reach a common understanding of our cultural failure and a common program for its reform, this gathering will be as vacuous and futile as many another solemn conclave of professors, advertised by high-sounding and promising titles.

But if I have stated the only purpose which might justify this Conference, then I must also say that it cannot possibly succeed. I do not bother to say that a conference, however good, cannot succeed in reforming modern culture, or even in correcting one of the main causes of its disorder, namely, modern education. That goes without saying. To expect such results would be to ask too much from even the best of all possible conferences. I mean, much more directly, that one cannot expect the professors to understand what is wrong with modern culture and modern education, for the simple reason that that would require them to understand what is wrong with their own mentality. If such a miracle could be hoped for, I would not be without hope for a peaceful deliverance from our manifold confusions. Since professors come to a conference of this sort with the intention of speaking their minds but not of changing them, with a willingness to listen but not to learn, with the kind of tolerance which delights in a variety of opinions and abominates the unanimity of agreement, it is preposterous to suppose that this Conference can even begin to realize the only ends which justify the enterprise.

Instead of a conference about science, philosophy and religion in relation to democracy, what is needed is a conference *about the professors* of science, philoso-

phy and religion, especially American professors whose intellectual attitudes express a false conception of democracy. The defects of modern culture are the defects of its intellectual leaders, its teachers and savants. The disorder of modern culture is a disorder in their minds, a disorder which manifests itself in the universities they have built, in the educational system they have devised, in the teaching they do, and which, through that teaching, perpetuates itself and spreads out in ever widening circles from generation to generation. It is a little naïve, therefore, to suppose that the professors can be called upon to solve the problem of the relationship of science, philosophy and religion in our education and in our culture —as naïve as it would be to invite the professors to participate in a conference about what is wrong with the professors.

We do not even have to wait until this Conference is over to discover its futility and the reasons therefor. The glorious, Quixotic failure of President Hutchins to accomplish any of the essential reforms which American education so badly needs, demonstrates the point for us. In fact, if he *could* have succeeded, this Conference would not be necessary now. The fact that he did not succeed may make this Conference necessary, in the sense that fundamental rectifications of modern culture are imperative; but if we understand why, in the nature of the situation, Hutchins could not succeed, we also see why a conference of professors about the defects of the modern mentality must be self-defeating.

What did Mr. Hutchins propose? He proposed, in the first place, that man is a rational animal, essentially distinct from the brutes, and hence, that education should cultivate the moral and the intellectual virtues. He proposed, in the second place, that science, philosophy and theology are distinct bodies of knowledge, radically different as to methods of knowing as well as with respect to objects known. But he went further. He said that theoretic philosophy delves more deeply into the nature of things than all the empirical sciences; that, as theoretic knowledge, philosophy is superior to the sciences by reason of the questions it can answer. He said that practical philosophy, dealing with ethical and political problems, is superior to applied science, because the latter at best gives us control over the physical means to be used, whereas practical philosophy determines the ends to be sought, and the ordering of all means thereto. Hence the structure of a university should not be a miscellaneous collection of departments from astronomy to zoology, with all treated as equally important theoretically and practically, but a hierarchy of studies, ordered educationally according to their intrinsic merits. Because of the fact that our secular universities harbor a diversity of religious faiths, Mr. Hutchins placed metaphysics at the summit instead of theology. For man the highest knowledge, and the most indispensable to his well-being, is the knowledge of God; and since the ultimate conclusions of metaphysics comprise a natural theology, metaphysics is the supreme subject-matter in the domain of natural knowledge. But Mr. Hutchins would have to admit (and he indicated his willingness to do so) that if there is a better knowledge of God, and man's relation to God, than metaphysics offers, then such knowledge is superior to philosophy, both theoretically and practically, just as philosophy is superior to science. Traditional Judaism and Christianity do, of course, claim that there is such knowledge, the sacred theology that rests on faith in God's revelation of Himself. It is properly distinguished from both science and philosophy as a supernatural knowledge, which man cannot have without God's direct aid.

Why did Mr. Hutchins fail? Anyone who has ever attended a faculty meeting knows the answer. It can be discovered by anyone who will read the reviews of *The Higher Learning in America*, written by the professors, or what is worse, the professional educators. He failed not because his analysis was patiently *demonstrated* to be in error; not because someone *proved* that philosophy does not exist or is inferior to science; or that religion is superstition, and sacred theology a rationalization of some make-believe. He failed because he was asking the professors to change their minds and to agree about something. He failed as much with the professors of philosophy as with the professors of science; he failed even more with those teachers of religion who regard themselves as liberal. What Hutchins proposed ran counter to every prejudice that constitutes the modern frame of mind, and its temper. The professors being in the vast majority, and ultimately controlling, *as they should,* educational policy, it was naïve of Mr. Hutchins to suppose that he could reform education by appealing to truths the professors ignored or denied. Worse than naïve, he had the effrontery to assume that if the professors were ignorant of certain truths or had neglected the implications of others, they would submit themselves to teaching on these points. Since the professors cannot conceive themselves as being taught, certainly not by anyone without a Ph.D. in their field, the man who tries to argue with the plain intention of winning agreement must really be trying to impose his doctrine. The simplest way to deal with a fellow like Hutchins is to call him a fascist.

Now I want to make one thing absolutely clear. I am not begging the question in this issue between Mr. Hutchins and his opponents, by proceeding as if I have proved the former right and the latter wrong. I know I have not proved the truth of any of the theses mentioned, nor have I proved the falsity of their contraries. With the time at my disposal that would be impossible to do under any circumstances; and even with much more time I would not try with this audience. With a few notable exceptions, the members of this Conference represent the American academic mind. It is that fact itself which makes it unnecessary, as well as unwise, for me to make any effort in the way of reasoning. I know too well, from such experience, the opinions of this audience, and of all the professors they represent — about the nature and relationship of science, philosophy and religion. I also know, because I have tried so many times to present an analysis with the fullest of supporting arguments, precisely what reactions such procedure calls forth. Fortunately, there is no need to verify this once again, because on this occasion I am concerned only to show the futility of a conference of professors about science, philosophy and religion.

That can be shown very simply. Either the prevailing opinions of the professors are right or they are wrong. Let us suppose, for the moment, that they are right, that what is now generally taught in American schools about the relation of science, philosophy and religion, is the true account. If it is true, there is nothing wrong with modern culture, for modern culture, in all its practices and institutions, embodies these opinions. On this alternative, therefore, it is difficult to see why there should be any conference about science, philosophy and religion. If, however, on the other alternative, the prevailing professorial opinions on these matters are wrong, and if, in addition, modern culture suffers grave disorders precisely because it embodies these opinions, then there is some point to a conference which would seek to correct the prevalent errors. But then it is pointless to ask the professors to consider the problem. They have already considered it and told us their answers in all their teaching and all their educational decisions. The same majority point of view will dominate this Conference, as in the Hutchins controversy. Of course, the minority view will get a hearing, with all that indifference about the truth which hides behind the mask of tolerance, but it is a foregone conclusion that nobody's mind will be changed; in fact, everyone knows that is not the aim of a conference, anyway. Hence, when all is said and done, the relative weights of majority and minority opinion will be registered once more. The Conference will have exhibited the characteristic mentality of our culture, and those who are deeply concerned about changing that mentality will be confirmed in their pessimism that nothing, simply nothing, can be done to reform our education or to reorient our culture.

Now I am well aware that my colleagues do not think there is any such clear-cut division between a majority and a minority view of science, philosophy and religion. For one thing, they do not like to acknowledge the existence of clear-cut issues, with truth on one side, and error on the other; if there were such issues, then anyone who undertook to think about them might be obliged to risk his academic reputation by coming to a definite conclusion. For another thing, the professors do not like to feel that they share even a common majority opinion with each other. The sacred individuality of each professor can be preserved only by differing. When one is in substantial sympathy with what a colleague has to say, he still safeguards his freedom of opinion by saying the same thing some other way. Most professors seem to feel that agreement, even if freely reached, violates their personal integrity.

Nevertheless, I charge the professors — and here I am speaking of the vast majority — with being in substantial agreement on one side of the crucial issues this Conference faces. I say that most of them are positivists. I know that there are enough varieties of positivism to permit the professors to retain their individuality, but I insist that behind the multiplicity of technical jargons there is a single doctrine. The essential point of that doctrine is simply the affirmation of science, and the denial of philosophy and religion. Again I am aware that the professors will smile at my simplicity. Whoever heard anyone, except a few violent extremists, flatly denying philosophy and religion; as a matter of fact, such dogmatic denials are made only by a small circle of "philosophers" who blatantly advertise themselves as positivists. The very presence at this Conference of scientists, philosophers and theologians shows that the representatives of the several disciplines respect each other; the fact that they are willing to listen to each other's papers shows the spirit of cooperation which prevails among them. One even begins to wonder about the sanity of those who talk about the disorder and disunity of modern culture. The real problem of this Conference must be the perils of Democracy; it certainly cannot be the issue about positivism.

Despite such blandishments, I repeat my charge. The professors, by and large, are positivists. And, furthermore, I say that the most serious threat to Democracy is the positivism of the professors, which dominates every aspect of modern education and is the central corruption of modern culture. Democracy has much more to fear from the mentality of its teachers than from the nihilism of Hitler. It is the same nihilism in both cases, but Hitler's is more honest and consistent, less blurred by subtleties and queasy qualifications, and hence less dangerous. I shall return to this point after I have supported my charge.

Within brief scope, the easiest way to force the professors into the open is by making the issues sharp and clear. Let me do this first with respect to philosophy, and then with respect to religion.

With respect to philosophy, the following propositions must be affirmed. He who denies any one of them denies philosophy. (1) Philosophy is public knowledge, not private opinion, in the same sense that science is knowledge, not opinion. (2) Philosophical knowledge answers questions which science cannot answer, now or ever, because its method is not adapted to answering such questions. (3) Because their methods are thus distinct, each being adapted to a different object of inquiry, philosophical and scientific knowledge are logically independent of one another, which means that the truth and falsity of philosophical principles or conclusions does not depend upon the changing content of scientific knowledge. (4) Philosophy is superior to science, both theoretically and practically: theoretically, because it is knowledge of the being of things whereas science studies only their phenomenal manifestations; practically, because philosophy establishes moral conclusions, whereas scientific knowledge yields only technological applications; this last point means that science can give us only a control over operable means, but it cannot make a single judgment about good and bad, right and wrong, in terms of the ends of human life. (5) There can be no conflict between scientific and philosophic truths, although philosophers may correct the errors of scientists who try to answer questions beyond their professional competence, just as scientists can correct the errors of philosophers guilty of a similar transgression. (6) There are no systems of philosophy, each of which may be considered true in its own way by criteria of internal consistency, each differing from the others, as so many systems of geometry, in terms of different origins in diverse, but equally arbitrary, postulates or definitions. (7) The first principles of all philosophical knowledge are metaphysical, and metaphysics is valid knowledge of both sensible and supra-sensible being. (8) Metaphysics is able to demonstrate the existence of supra-sensible being, for it can demonstrate the existence of God, by appealing to the evidence of the senses and the principles of reason, and without any reliance upon articles of religious faith.

These eight propositions are not offered as an exhaustive account of the nature of philosophy, its distinction from, and relation to, science. I have chosen them simply because they will serve like intellectual litmus paper to bring out the acid of positivism. Let the professors who claim to respect philosophy — and this goes as much for the professors of philosophy as for the others — decide whether they affirm every one of these propositions. Those who say that philosophy is just another kind of knowledge but not superior to science might just as well call philosophy opinion and deny its existence. Those who suppose that philosophical principles or conclusions are

dependent on the findings of science; those who suppose that real technical competence is necessary in order to solve scientific problems, whereas none is needed for philosophical problems; those who think that philosophy comprises a variety of logically constructed systems, among which you can take your choice according to your preference among postulates; those who say philosophy is all right, but metaphysics is nonsense, and there is no rational knowledge of God — all these deny philosophy. They are positivists. If the professors were clear of mind and forthright of speech, they would come right out and say that they regard philosophy as opinion, not knowledge. But professors are unaccustomed to simple affirmations and denials. They give true-false tests, but never take them. They will, therefore, avoid the test I have presented by saying that it is all a matter of how you use words, or that it all depends on your point of view, or something equally evasive. Yet, by their evasions shall you know them, for those who affirm philosophy to be knowledge neither hesitate nor quibble on any of these points.

With respect to religion, the following propositions must be affirmed. He who denies any one of them denies religion, in any sense which makes it distinct in character from science and philosophy. (1) Religion involves knowledge of God and of man's destiny, knowledge which is not naturally acquired in the sense in which both science and philosophy are natural knowledge. (2) Religious faith, on which sacred theology rests, is itself a supernatural act of the human intellect, and is thus a Divine gift. (3) Because God is its cause, faith is more certain than knowledge resulting from the purely natural action of the human faculties. (4) What is known by faith about God's nature and man's destiny is knowledge which exceeds the power of the human intellect to attain without God's revelation of Himself and His Providence. (5) Sacred theology is independent of philosophy, in that its principles are truths of faith, whereas philosophical principles are truths of reason, but this does not mean that theology can be speculatively developed without reason serving faith. (6) There can be no conflict between philosophical and theological truths, although theologians may correct the errors of philosophers who try to answer questions beyond the competence of natural reason, just as philosophers can correct the errors of theologians who violate the autonomy of reason. (7) Sacred theology is superior to philosophy, both theoretically and practically: theoretically, because it is more perfect knowledge of God and His creatures; practically, because moral philosophy is insufficient to direct man to God as his last end. (8) Just as there are no systems of philosophy, but only philosophical knowledge less or more adequately possessed by different men, so there is only one true religion, less or more adequately embodied in the existing diversity of creeds.

These eight propositions, like those concerning philosophy, are far from exhaustive. They are intended simply as a device to bring professorial positivism — or shall I call it "negativism?"— out into the open. Those who claim to respect the distinct place of religion in modern culture, but refuse to grant that religion rests upon supernatural knowledge, or that it is superior to both philosophy and science, either know not what they say or are guilty of profound hypocrisy. For unless religion involves supernatural knowledge, it has no separate status whatsoever; and if it rests upon supernatural knowledge, it must be accorded

the supreme place in the cultural hierarchy. Religion cannot be regarded as just another aspect of culture, one among many human occupations, of indifferent importance along with science and art, history and philosophy. Religion is either the supreme human discipline, because it is God's discipline of man, and as such dominates our culture, or it has no place at all. The mere toleration of religion, which implies indifference to or denial of its claims, produces a secularized culture as much as militant atheism or Nazi nihilism. Philosophers who think that all the significant questions men ask are either answerable by reason or not at all, are naturalists in a sense analogous to the positivism of scientists who think that science alone is valid knowledge, and that science is enough for the conduct of life. If the professors are positivists, they are certainly naturalists. They dishonor themselves as well as religion by tolerating it when, all equivocations overcome, they really think that faith is superstition, just as they think philosophy is opinion. The kind of positivism and naturalism which is revealed in all their works and all their teaching, is at the root of modern secularized culture. . . .

I have so far pointed out the significance of this Conference for the state of our culture, and the doom it forebodes. In conclusion, I wish to indicate briefly the bearing of my analysis upon the crisis of Democracy. Let me say at once that I hold Democracy to be the greatest political good, the most perfect form of political community; and I hold this not as a matter of fine feeling or local opinion, but because I think it is a conclusion which can be demonstrated in terms of the truths of moral and political philosophy. Now, what can positivists say about such a demonstration? Obviously, they must repudiate it. Outside the sphere of science nothing can be demonstrated, and the proposition that Democracy is the *best* political order certainly lies outside the sphere of science. What is neither self-evident nor demonstrable must be an opinion, which attracts or repels us emotionally. Anyone who denies that philosophy is knowledge denies, of course, the self-evidence of moral principles and the validity of moral demonstrations. Hence the professors can be for Democracy only because they like it, not because they know it is right. They talk a great deal about natural rights and the dignity of man, but this is loose and irresponsible talk, in which they lightly indulge because they do not mind contradicting themselves. There are no natural rights if there is no natural moral law, which is binding upon all men everywhere in the same way. Man has no dignity if he is not a rational animal, essentially distinct from the brutes by reason of the spiritual dimension of his being. This should be enough to make clear that positivists are forced to deny the rights and dignity of man, or hold such views only as prejudice, rationally no better than Hitler's prejudices to the contrary. But to reinforce the point that the professors have no grounds for any of their fine feelings, let me add that the same facts which warrant man's dignity as an end to be served by the state also imply that man has an immortal soul, and a destiny beyond the temporal order. In short, one cannot have reasons for affirming Democracy and at the same time deny the truths of philosophy and religion.

Of course, the sort of democracy to which the professors are sentimentally attached cannot be demonstrably approved, for theirs is an essentially false conception. The social order they would like to preserve is the anarchic individual-ism, the corrupt liberalism, which is the most vicious caricature of Democracy. Objecting to any inequalities in value, objecting to any infringement of absolute individual liberty by loyalties and obligations to superior goods, they want a democracy without hierarchy and without authority. In short, they want chaos, not order, a society in which everyone will be as free as if he lived alone, a community in which common bonds will not bind the individual at all. Even when they speak enthusiastically about this false ideal, the professors seldom claim that they have rational grounds for its defense. The very fact that they so frequently refer to democracy, not as a government or as a political order, but as a way of life, reveals them as exponents of a false religion. This religion of democracy is no better than the religion of fascism. One is the idolatry of individual liberty as the other is the worship of collective might.

One of the greatest achievements of the modern world is the discovery of the moral and political reasons for the democratic ideal, as well as actual experimentation in the field of democratic processes. But though it be in this sense a child of modern times, Democracy will not be fully achieved until modern culture is radically reformed. Science contributes nothing whatsoever to the understanding of Democracy. Without the truths of philosophy and religion, Democracy has no rational foundation. In America at present it is at best a cult, a local prejudice, a traditional persuasion. Today it is challenged by other cults which seem to have more might, and no less right, so far as American ability to defend democracy rationally is concerned.

For all these reasons I say we have more to fear from our professors than from Hitler. It is they who have made

American education what it is, both in content and method: in content, an indoctrination of positivism and naturalism; in method, an exhibition of anarchic individualism masquerading as the democratic manner. Whether Hitler wins or not, the culture which is formed by such education cannot support what democracy we have against interior decay.

If I dared to raise my voice as did the prophets in ancient Israel, I would ask whether the tyrants of today are not like the Babylonian and Assyrian kings — instruments of Divine justice, chastening a people who had departed from the way of truth. In the inscrutable Providence of God, and according to the nature of man, a civilization may sometimes reach a rottenness which only fire can expunge and cleanse. If the Babylonians and Assyrians were destroyers, they were also deliverers. Through them, the prophets realized, God purified His people. Seeing the hopelessness of working peaceful reforms among a people who had shut their eyes and hardened their hearts, the prophets almost prayed for such deliverance, through the darkness of destruction, to the light of a better day. So, perhaps, the Hitlers in the world today are preparing the agony through which our culture shall be reborn. Certainly if it is a part of the Divine plan to bless man's temporal civilization with the goodness of Democracy, that civilization must be rectified. It is probably not from Hitler, but from the professors, that we shall ultimately be saved.

Sidney Hook: THE NEW MEDIEVALISM

WE have just been told that American democracy is in greater danger from its professors than from Hitlerism. Such a statement is not merely false but irresponsible, and at the present time, doubly so. I do not know whether it has been uttered with an eye to making newspaper headlines; it cannot have been uttered by anyone who respects the truth. Consider, for a moment, what that statement implies. Hitlerism represents the most ruthless system of physical and spiritual terror since the days of the crusade against the Albigensian heresy, and of the medieval inquisition. Hitler has crucified an entire people, uprooted and destroyed millions of lives throughout Europe, outraged every value of liberal civilization which we Americans hold dear. If our professors are worse than Hitler, presumably they threaten us with worse than this — but the only crime which Mr. Adler has been able to convict them of is differing with him (and President Hutchins). The consequences of differing with Mr. Adler are so grave, that they lead him to assert that "until the professors and their culture are liquidated, the resolution of modern problems will not even begin."

Why should our differences with Mr. Adler be so fateful? Because, forsooth,

Reprinted by permission from the *New Republic*, CIII, No. 18 (October 28, 1940), 602–606. [The following comments were delivered by Professor Sidney Hook of New York University on the paper by Mortimer Adler, reproduced on page 67. Ed.]

our professors, like Hitler, are *positivists*. Now whatever the definition of philosophical positivism is, there is no evidence at all that it is the cause, or even among the chief causes, of the rise of Hitlerism abroad and of the dangers of totalitarianism at home. The question of the causes of fascism in Italy and Germany, and the question of the causes of the present world war against democracy (which began with the antipositivistic rebellion of Franco, aided by Hitler and Mussolini, against Spanish democracy), are empirical *historical* questions. They are not questions of metaphysics or theology. I am acquainted with no *scientific* historian who has asserted that the rise of Hitlerism is due to a philosophical doctrine rather than to the conjunction of economic depression, the consequences of the Treaty of Versailles, the errors in policy of democratic parties within Germany and of the democratic governments without. After all, it is precisely the cultures which Mr. Adler himself damns as positivistic, England and America, which are leading the fight against Hitler and Mussolini instead of making concordats with them as some antipositivistic organizations have done.

We have here a crass illustration of how, in the interests of metaphysical dogma, Mr. Adler can subvert empirical truth. And this despite his lip recognition of the autonomy of scientific inquiry. Throughout his paper, wherever Mr. Adler touches upon questions for which *evidence* is available, what he says is inadequate or clearly false.

I have time for only brief observations on this point before going on to his main position. One of the reasons why Mr. Adler believes it "unnecessary as well as unwise to make any effort in the way of reasoning" with this conference is the critical reception which the American academic mind has given to the writings of President Hutchins. According to Mr. Adler, that reception was abusive and ignorant, not intelligently critical in the slightest. Nothing can be further from the truth. President Hutchins' book[1] received adequate hearing and review. Without defending current educational practices, this criticism established that President Hutchins' views were historically false, badly reasoned in a succession of arguments containing undistributed middle terms, and pernicious in their conclusions. Of several such criticisms I cite only that of John Dewey, and the subsequent exchange between him and President Hutchins, in which the latter literally abandoned the field after failing to meet a single point raised in Professor Dewey's courteous but searching analysis.[2]

Or take Mr. Adler's charge that the modern professor "will not subject himself to the rigors of public disputation." If by disputation we mean the public, critical analysis of ideas in order to achieve clarification and to determine what evidence would be relevant to the truth of meaningful assertions, then I submit that Mr. Adler's charge is plainly false. Although practice may fall short of the ideal in many respects, this is precisely the aim of those professional associations and periodicals which carry on the intellectual enterprise in American life. But if by public disputation we mean denunciation of all who do not hold our alleged "self-evident" truths instead of analysis of them, and calculated insults under the guise of plain speaking, coupled with a call for liquidation of heretics in metaphysics and theology —

[1] Robert M. Hutchins, *The Higher Learning in America* (New Haven, 1936).

[2] *Cf. Social Frontier*, Jan., Feb., March, 1937.

of which Mr. Adler has just given us an illustration — then I am happy that, in the main, our nonparochial intellectual life is free of it.

I leave to those who have initiated this conference the reply to Mr. Adler's attack upon its purpose. I wish rather to say a word about Mr. Adler's series of propositions in metaphysics and theology, every one of which, he holds, is entailed by rational belief in democracy, so that a difference with him on any point is tantamount to a denial of democracy. I begin with the metaphysical propositions. Mr. Adler in advance has ruled out as evasive any reply to his propositions which would make their truth or falsity depend upon the meaning assigned to his words, i.e., upon the distinctions in the sense and uses of his key terms. He demands yes or no answers. Now true-false answers to isolated propositions may be demanded in religious catechisms. They cannot be intelligently given to philosophical questions without *analysis*. And the wisdom of philosophical analysis, from the time of Aristotle down, consists just in this ability to make distinctions in the meaning and use of terms before essaying an answer to them.

However, if I understand what Mr. Adler means by his key terms (and in order not to disappoint him), I categorically declare, speaking only for myself, that all of his propositions are false, and further that, true or false, they do not entail, except by arbitrary definition, any political view whatsoever. Behind these propositions in metaphysics lie a number of unexamined assumptions, upon which they depend. The first is that no warranted assertion can be made unless it ultimately depends upon some absolute indemonstrable truth of reason or indisputable truth of sense-perception or both;

the second is that these truths are grasped immediately and intuitively; the third is the belief that things have essential natures, distinct from what are called their accidents, and that only the former, in contradistinction to the concerns of modern science, are the proper subject of knowledge. There are many other assumptions upon which Mr. Adler's metaphysical propositions rest. These assumptions may justify a belief in necessary, self-evident truths about the world and man, but they are themselves not self-evident. Yet despite the fact that all of Mr. Adler's certainties, immediate or derived, rest upon highly dubitable assumptions, he asserts that those who deny any *one* of his propositions are denying philosophy. Since there is no leading figure in modern philosophy, whether it be Descartes, Locke, Spinoza, Kant, who has not denied at least one of Mr. Adler's propositions, the preposterous implication is that there is no such thing as modern philosophy and that most of those who are called philosophers are but blind and wicked nominalists.

It is not surprising, therefore, that Mr. Adler speaks so scornfully of the contingent and tentative character of scientific knowledge, contrasting it with the *superior* knowledge of metaphysics and theology. For the progress of scientific knowledge flies full in the face of every one of his assumptions about the nature of knowledge, so that Mr. Adler is logically compelled to dismiss science as *mere opinion* about phenomena, incapable of giving us truth about the "real" nature of things.

Logical analysis of scientific method shows that no scientific proposition, whether as premise or conclusion, postulate or law, rule or description, is self-evident. Every proposition must justify itself, and no vicious infinite regress is involved because the solution of genuine problems, through the acquisition of piecemeal knowledge, controls inquiry. What all justifications of the assertion of scientific statements have in common is this: reference to the verifiable consequences of their use and not to antecedent certainties. Mr. Adler's metaphysics rules itself out of court when it rules out scientific knowledge as genuine knowledge, or gives it an inferior status to ontological or theological knowledge.

There is irony in the fact that more universal *agreement* exists about scientific ideas, which make no pretense of being self-evidently true, than about any axioms or self-evident truths which have ever been advanced at any time by any metaphysical school. The moral is that we ought to extend scientific method to the questions and problems in social life about which there is *disagreement*.

As for Mr. Adler's self-evident or derived metaphysical truths, in so far as meaning can be assigned them, I am convinced it can be shown that where they are not false they are either tautologies, rules of discourse or disguised definitions, or, at best, vague empirical generalizations on a commonsense level which can be better established by the more precise methods of science. And despite Mr. Adler's excommunication of all who disagree with him, I believe it is still possible to be a philosopher without subscribing to *his* philosophy.

I come now to Mr. Adler's theological propositions. Time permits a discussion of only one proposition, the final one which asserts "Just as there are no systems of philosophy, but only philosophical knowledge less or more adequately possessed by different men, so there is only one true religion, less or more adequately embodied in the existing diversity of creeds." According to Mr. Adler,

this is another proposition which, if *denied*, entails the denial of all religion, the negation of democracy, and a nihilism that is as bad as Hitler's. But it is clear that if it is *affirmed*, then the members of *all* religions other than the true religion differ only in the degree of their positivism from Hitler. For on Mr. Adler's hierarchical scheme, religions are ordered in the scale of their approximation to the one true religion, and no one is without some religion even if it be the religion of Satan. From the point of view of that *one true* religion, all the others represent a graded variety in the abominations of positivist heresy. The primary question, then, is to determine which is the true religion. There are grounds for suspecting that Mr. Adler believes he has the supernatural knowledge that constitutes the answer. Given his view that those who deny this truth are positivists, and that positivists are an even greater danger than Hitler (because Hitler, says Mr. Adler, is an honest man), it follows that, like the positivist professors, those who hold any religion but the true religion should be liquidated for the good of their own souls, if they cannot be converted to the truth. Whether Mr. Adler is aware of it or not — and I sometimes think he has not yet learned how to read his own words — this constitutes a justification of religious intolerance.

I am not forcing an interpretation upon Mr. Adler's paper, although he will probably make that claim. These are the logical implications of his remarks. They are confirmed by what he has to say of the cultural beauties of medieval culture, of which the liquidation of religious heresy and the Inquisition were integral parts, and his belief that positivism, the root of all modern evil, began with the Renaissance and Reformation and culminated in Hitlerism. Just as Hitler

would like to undo the Treaty of West-
phalia, which recognized freedom of religious conscience, so Mr. Adler and
those who think as he does would like
to undo the Renaissance, the Reformation, the French Revolution and the subsequent trend toward democratic secu-
larism which makes the state neutral
in religion.

In effect, Mr. Adler is proposing, in
the terminology of metaphysics and theology and in the protective coloration of
a democrat, that the members of this
Conference, assembled to defend and
further the democratic way of life against
the menace of totalitarianism, adjourn
their fight against Hitlerism — and fight
each other. As opposed to Mr. Adler, I
do not believe that there is any such
thing as a philosophical fifth-column. But
if there *were* anything that could possibly be regarded as such, then I believe
that it could be demonstrated that it
would be not positivism but the views
of Mr. Adler.

Mr. Adler is entitled to defend his
views, wrong as I believe them to be.
We can only request that in the interests
of truth and fruitful intellectual procedure, of which he asserts this conference
has no conception, he argue his position
instead of begging it and refrain from
distorting the views of those with whom
he disagrees. It is intellectually cheap,
for example, to assert, as Mr. Adler does,
that because democrats reject a society
with *his* conception of hierarchy and
authority, they want "chaos, not order";

"anarchic individualism," not healthy
social relations.

One word in conclusion. Mr. Adler believes that the fact that "the minority
view," meaning his own, gets a hearing
at this conference indicates our "indifference about the truth which hides behind
the mask of tolerance." I hope I speak
for others besides myself when I say
that it is not indifference to the truth but
the love of truth, and the reasonable faith
of reasonable men which leads us to give
a hearing to those with whom we disagree. Tolerance is a mask only when
those who profess it await the day when
they will be sufficiently strong to eliminate heretical differences on fundamental
questions. Tolerance toward ideas, with
the hope of learning and with the privi-
lege of rejecting (or suspending judgment) on the basis of evidence, is of the
very lifeblood of democracy.

The history of science shows that it is
possible to keep an open house to ideas,
and at the same time to build up a great
body of reliable knowledge commanding
universal agreement. This has been done
without any authority except the volun-
tarily accepted authority of method —
reason and experiment — without a Ges-
tapo or GPU or Inquisition, without an
Index of proscribed books or doctrines,
and finally, without the dogma of final
and absolute truths. Our hope lies in
building the values and attitudes of
scientific method more firmly into the
living tissues of the democratic way of
life.

Howard Selsam: SCIENCE AND ETHICS

DURING the second Roosevelt ad- ministration a series of conferences was held by the Department of Agricul- ture with groups of leaders in the social sciences — economists, political scientists, historians, anthropologists, sociologists, and social psychologists. At these con- ferences, questions of the desirable ob- jectives of our national society and of rural life in particular came up for dis- cussion, but the social scientists chose to ignore these questions. They did so on the ground that as scientists they could be concerned only with problems of fact, while questions of objectives or ends be- long in the sphere of values and thus are the special property of philosophy and religion. Accordingly, the Department called in philosophers and religious lead- ers to solve the problem of the objectives of American agriculture.

This may seem like a peculiar division of labor to the unsophisticated, but it represents a strong and respected tradi- tion in modern thought. Scientists, this tradition runs, deal only with questions of fact, with what is the case, with the world and human society merely as it *is*. They can also predict what *will* happen if a certain experiment is performed or a certain course of action embarked upon. But, the theory goes, they neither can nor should attempt to deal with values, that is, with what ought to be the case, with what course of action is desirable, or with what constitutes a good life. Phi- losophy and religion, on the contrary, are presumably preoccupied purely with values rather than with what is the case.

Philosophers and theologians may be ignorant, from a scientific standpoint, of the nature of the world, of men, and of social and economic processes, but they reputedly know what men *ought* to be and what the ideal life is.

This divorce of fact and value, and of the two groups who specialize in each, appears even more perverse when viewed in concrete detail. The social scientists, for example, can compute how many of those who raise our crops own the land they till. They can determine the relative efficiency of sharecropping and of other forms of farming, the causes of soil ero- sion and its effects on the farm popula- tion, the relatively lower intelligence quotients of children in rural areas as compared with those of city children, the effect of an impoverished diet on health, the rate of growth of mechanization of American agriculture with its resultant increase in production per farmer and the accompanying separation of hun- dreds of thousands of farm families from the soil they had previously tilled. They can also determine, by rigorously scien- tific means, the major needs of our rural population with regard to housing, cloth- ing, food, and the like, as well as what they need in educational and cultural services to bring them up to the level of city dwellers of moderate incomes. One would think that this alone could occupy the social scientists for some time to come, without their having to appeal to philosophy and religion. Why then, do they make this divorce between what *is* and what *ought to be?* Was Professor

From *Socialism and Ethics* by Howard Selsam. International Publishers Co., Inc., 1943. Reprinted by permission.

Morris R. Cohen correct when he answered this question by saying, "Those who boast that they are not, as social scientists, interested in what ought to be, generally assume (tacitly) that the hitherto prevailing order is the proper ideal of what ought to be?"

How can philosophers and religious leaders determine "the desirable objectives of our national society or our rural life?" They must do so by deduction from some abstract principles concerning either man's ultimate good in this world or the prerequisites for his salvation in the next, or else they must become social scientists and seek to do the job that those who are technically better trained and equipped have so woefully neglected. Is there any alternative to the scientific determination of values in any given place and time, by a thorough knowledge of existing conditions, of men's needs and desires, and of the actual processes whereby these may be fulfilled, other than that of speculation concerning what men *ought* to desire or how they *ought* to live? And is there not danger that such speculation will be derived from *a priori* principles concerning the nature of man and his goals — principles based upon the interests of a ruling class, present or past?

Few will deny that men's needs and desires, and the means of fulfilling them, the ways whereby men can control themselves and their environment are possible and actual objects of scientific knowledge. Yet outside of Marxism there exist the greatest confusion and a predominant attitude that somehow science and value judgments are hopelessly and forever distinct, if not actually irreconcilable. And where attempts at harmony are sought, the technique is mainly idealistic, proceeding to make all science anthropomorphic and to sow values broadcast throughout the world of nature. This approach gives the illusion of solving the problem, but only by denying the objective validity of scientific method and its fruits.[1] The roots of this separation of fact and value lie deep within the bourgeois system and its world view. It is safe to say that the opposition would never have arisen if the developing bourgeoisie had not found it necessary to compromise the science it required for its commerce, metallurgy, and technology generally, with those elements of the old religion that were both useful for keeping the masses quiet and for justifying its system of private ownership and profit. In the most militant and progressive stages of the rise of the bourgeoisie, its philosophers sought to create a moral science, but, as we shall try to show, they were doomed to failure by the impossibility of reconciling the actual processes of capitalist economy with the needs and aspirations of the masses of men.

An illustration of the unfortunate consequences of the current separation of science and value and the resultant division of labor between scientists and *philosophers* is the report of the Philosophy Conference held by the U. S. Department of Agriculture.[2] A representative group of American professors of philosophy attended the conference, together with representatives of the Department. Under the heading of "Desirable Objectives of Rural Life," a number of principles were agreed upon by the conferees. The first was that "the *security of land tenure* — whether in the form of relatively unencumbered ownership or long-lease tenancy — is essential to the well-being of farm life." Clearly, the

[1] See, for example, Wolfgang Köhler, *The Place of Value in a World of Facts.*

[2] *Philosophy Conference on Agriculture* (U. S. Department of Agriculture, May 29, 1939).

phrase "relatively unencumbered ownership" has no scientific definiteness. How many mortgages does this allow, how much of the farmer's income may go to interest payments? Long-lease tenancy may give security of tenure but under what terms and at what costs to the living standards of the farm family? And how conducive to the realization of the next recommendation is any tenant farm system — whether the owner himself lives and farms nearby, or is a bank or insurance company in a distant urban center?

The second recommendation is that there be stimulated "a greater responsibility," a "moral responsibility" "to *preserve our land resources* on behalf of the national welfare." To this end, the philosophers say, there should be invigorated in the nation "a healthy sentiment which may yet develop into a patriotism of the soil — a fair equivalent in the United States of the peasant attachments that characterize the older world from which our populations have sprung." Again it must be asked how tenant farmers can get this "patriotism of the soil," this concern with protecting the land they till, which is not now and can perhaps never become their own? Compare such a recommendation with the concrete situation of agriculture in America as presented fictionally but concretely in *The Grapes of Wrath*, or scientifically and analytically in Anna Rochester's *Why Farmers Are Poor*. Nothing is said by the philosophers about sharecropping, about the vast land holdings of the insurance companies, about the colossal gap between the prices the farmer receives for his products and the prices paid by the city consumer for processed agricultural commodities. And, similarly, not a word is said about the inevitable abuse of the soil that goes with the backward agricultural set-up of large parts of the South,

with their single-crop economy and the desire on the part of owning corporations to wring every last cent of profit from the soil each year. Fact and value are completely dissociated, and the inevitable result is the conversion of a scientific social problem into a problem of "moral responsibility," and an objective, natural, rational concern on the part of tillers of the soil with the future of their land into a mystical "patriotism of the soil" for which more backward European economies are taken as the model.

The third recommendation ignores actual conditions even more, and as a consequence has more definitely reactionary and fascist implications. Its thesis is that the country offers "the maximum opportunities for *realizing the normal cycle of human life*." Suggestive of the French anarcho-syndicalist, Georges Sorel, whose philosophy influenced Mussolini and fascist ideology generally, is the philosophers' emphasis on the rural home as "central to the desirable type of life," and as "developing a distinctive and invaluable frame of mind." This is a reactionary point of view inasmuch as it is based on the *permanent* separation of rural from urban life and the glorification of the economically and culturally backward rural home. Further, it points toward the development and maintenance of a distinctively "peasant" mentality as an ideal. Logically carrying out this idea, the conferees extol "the increasing self-subsistence on the farm, as regards food, clothing, and shelter," and "the improvement of home conditions, by intelligent work rather than by the expenditure of money." The true reason for this approach is found in the following sentence of the report, where regard is expressed for "the rounded human expectation of life, for owner, tenant, and the hired help as well." In short, the existing capitalist frame-work of American agriculture must remain untouched and *values* can only be sought within the very class relationships that have created the capitalist *agrarian problem*. A scientific examination would reveal the need for a radical reconstruction of American agricultural relations: the elimination of owner, tenant, hired-help relationships; the completest possible mechanization of all agricultural processes; the integration of farm and urban communities through economic and cultural exchange on equal terms, and thereby the breaking down of the existing distinctions and cleavages between urban and rural life.

All of the above provides an appalling example of what happens when scientific analysis and moral evaluation are separated through a division of labor — when the scientific investigation of a situation in terms of actual human needs and possibilities is shunted from its proper course. The result is that moral judgments of "philosophers" are substituted for scientific analysis, actual conditions are ignored, and the concrete means whereby human needs can be fulfilled in accordance with technological developments are neglected. Social scientists alone can solve such a problem, but only when out of loyalty to science they are willing to free themselves from the shackles of existing economic relationships; only when they include in their sphere the whole domain of human needs and the possibility of their fulfillment provided by the control of the forces of production, both industrial and agricultural, which modern society has attained. But to do this means to be *radical*, to go to the roots of the problem and ask: What changes in economic (class) relationships are necessary if our rural population is to have the fruits of modern industrial development and its resultant increased cultural possibilities, and if the urban communities are to possess the full fruit of the soil modern technology makes possible?

Opposed to this division of science and ethics is the Deweyan philosophy, which holds that science, reason, *intelligence* can solve all problems. According to those who hold this theory, if we would only use the "method of intelligence," as opposed apparently to *force*, all difficulties would be solved. But their science is a pseudo-science that categorically eliminates from the picture the actual nature of men and of existing social forces. Thus it operates in a theoretical vacuum. The difference between John Brown with all his faults and the general run of Abolitionists lay in the fact that he recognized that the force of the slave-owners on the side of evil would go down only before a superior force on the side of justice and right. And the slave-owners rebellion in 1861 proved the correctness of Brown's understanding. The science or intelligence that could have solved the slavery problem in the United States could only have been a science that recognized that two social orders were by their own inherent nature engaged in mortal combat, that the systems of slave labor and of free labor could not continue to exist side by side, and that no amount of reasoning could solve the slavery problem. Applied to the agricultural situation in America today, this means that either *science* must take the position it so often takes, that it has nothing to do with the ends sought but only with descriptions of conditions actually existing, or it must deal with the *whole* problem in terms of the needs of the urban and rural populations, with the possibilities modern technological developments offer for both agriculture and industry, and with the forces that prevent these possibilities from being realized. Dewey's whole approach is tantamount to the denial of class conflict and of irreconcilable social forces. Thus it affirms the basic rationality of the capitalist order.

The inadequacy and subtly reactionary nature of the Deweyan approach gives us a clue concerning the preconditions for the scientific determination of values or, in other words, for a science of ethics. First, paradoxically, there must be agreement on the desired ends of human social life, such, for example, as health and shelter, reproduction and recreation, security and sanity, and an ever-expanding richness of experience, for *all the people*. But does not this agreement presuppose a *moral* judgment that is not itself scientifically arrived at? It is precisely here that historical materialism, the Marxist science of society and history, or more exactly, the science of the ever-changing history of society, enters. If the controlling factor in the evolution of society is the development of the forces of production, and if these forces can develop only by supplying more people with ever more of the material necessities and goods of life, then it follows that the scientifically determinable direction of social development is towards this end. Slave society arose and gave way to feudalism, feudalism to capitalism, and capitalism, in part of the world, to socialism, and in each transition the moral ideals that arose were themselves generated out of the historical process, and reacted upon it. And within these larger patterns of economic relations similar movements occurred, such, for example, as the transition from mercantilism to *laissez-faire* capitalism

and from that to monopoly capitalism. The direction of development, except for artificial and ultimately unsuccessful attempts to check and stifle them is towards increased productive facilities and their fuller use. But this is possible only with greater consumption, with an ever-widening market, which requires an improved standard of living for wider masses of people. All that tends in this direction or allows for the possibility of such development can thus scientifically be called progressive, and all that militates against it is reactionary.

When we apply this historical materialist method to American agriculture today we see at once how meaningless is the attempt of the "philosophers" to formulate "the desirable ends of our rural life" without a scientific study of the whole economic scene and how thoroughly unscientific is the position of the social scientists and they cannot concern themselves with the values of rural life. At the present writing an interesting insight is provided into this problem by the concern of Nazi spokesmen with the Soviet collective farms in the territory still occupied by the German armies. To keep them, they say, is to allow socialism, which is intolerable, and to seek to break them up and restore individual farming under conditions of mechanization is to reduce seriously the productive capacity of the farms so necessary to Nazi war economy. In short, the collective farm is scientifically desirable but socially and politically incompatible with the capitalist economic structure.

What the social scientists really mean when they say they can only describe facts and not determine objectives is that if they were to recommend the changes in the economic relationships necessary for agriculture to attain the productivity that science and technology now make possible, they would come into conflict with capitalist economy.

To sum up, science can operate in the value sphere and can determine values only if all can and do agree that the values of human life are scientifically determinable. And the precondition for this agreement is a scientific theory of history and society. In other words, if we take a completely scientific materialist approach to human life, then science and ethics are harmonious, and if we do not, then they are necessarily and forever at odds. The present dilemma of existing bourgeois theory lies in the fact that if the capitalist world used a thoroughly scientific standard it would have to abdicate. It does, to be sure, use scientific methods to determine its accepted values, profit, maintenance of the profit system, and so on, but it cannot apply them, with the exception of a war situation, to the determination of wider goods and must hence deny that there can be agreement on what these goods are. Thus it is that bourgeois philosophy can offer as the solution of all problems only the inacceptable alternatives of "logical positivism"—that science and value are unrelated — or of pragmatism, with its vague and abstract talk of the "method of intelligence.". . .

What social scientists really mean when they say they cannot tell what ought to be, but only how given objectives might be attained, is that they refuse to indicate remedies and directives with regard to ascertained or ascertainable needs that go beyond existing economic frameworks. But, and this can be shown by innumerable concrete references, they can also tell perfectly easily by scientific techniques where both real needs and actually desired ends come

into conflict with these existing economic structures.

All of this raises the age-old question of the relation of needs and desires. Treated idealistically, as it generally was, it too often remained a mere opposition between what an individual, a class, or a people in general wanted, and what someone thought they *ought* to want. But in more and more spheres we have reached the possibility, if not the actuality, of determining what men ought to want in terms of what they actually need within the possibility of scientific determination. Most animals, in a state of nature, exhibit a remarkable parallel between what they need for their life and preservation and what they seek. But with man and the animals he has domesticated there is only too often no such direct relationship.

Dr. Kurt Richter of John Hopkins University worked on one phase of this problem with rats. He set up what has been called his "cafeteria system" whereby the rats choose from separate sources the amount of various separate elements required and not required for their diet. He found a remarkably close correlation between what they needed, even under special conditions determined in advance, and what they selected in their "cafeteria." In man, due to the greater range of his appetites, his early social environment, and so on, there is relatively little such correlation. But this too can be scientifically determined. We *do* know certain foods that are good for children and adults but that they may not like nearly so much as other foods that are not only not required by their systems but inimical to their proper physical development. We can show equally objectively that certain sanitary conditions are needed that people "naturally" (which, of course, always remains determined by a particular social environment) not only might not seek but actually rebel against. Education, for example, has sometimes had to be *compulsory*, not to mention inoculation against smallpox, or needed precautions in cases of epidemics such as the forced quarantine system. Similarly, it is not too fantastic to suggest that there are cultural needs, in the sense of requirements under given conditions for the development of healthy and stable personalities, that can be empirically arrived at, and that may run against opposed desires under certain conditions. When we look at our whole educational system, this appears as a truism, but it is little enough reflected in our theories of the "good" and its scientific determinability.

The chief reason, obviously, for this conflict, is to be found in the fact that what people need is one thing and what the dominant economic class would like them to desire is something different. It is so different, in fact, that it not only cannot be determined scientifically, but runs counter to any scientific approach. Thus Monsignor Fulton J. Sheen finds that "labor, in its quest for social justice, is in danger of stressing the wrong thing — security, rather than the Christian principle of liberty."[3] The significant feature of his argument is that the "Christian principle of liberty" is identified with the private ownership of property. But inasmuch as the dominant form of property today is the ownership of the means of production it is this that Monsignor Sheen is equating with Christian liberty. In similar vein we find Roger W. Babson, the oracle of the stock exchange, saying: "If they (the unemployed) can't climb

out after being helped, they should fail — that is nature's method of showing them they are wrong. The WPA is a hospital for inefficient people." These spokesmen for big business criticize the people's desires in relation not to the needs of the people but to the needs of the capitalist system. Workers *want and need* security and the unemployed *want and need* jobs, so that the problem is not one of conflicting desires and needs but of conflicting *class* interests and needs.

This problem brings up sharply the reason for the fact that there can be no bourgeois science of values: namely, that there is no ultimate community of interests between the class that owns the instruments of production and the class that operates them. And not only is there no economic community (as opposed, for example, to a common national interest); there is not even indifference, for a worker's gain is a capitalist's loss, just as in the long run the opposite holds. Interests may be in community, hostile, or just indifferent. Here they are directly hostile, or in contradiction. Spinoza clearly saw this distinction when he stressed that in so far as men are guided by reason they seek things they can all have, but when they follow their passions they seek goals that by their nature some can have only at the expense of others. Since this is the case in the capitalist world, a capitalist science of values is impossible. The working class, on the other hand, by its very position in the productive process can have such a science, since its existence does not require the existence of capitalists — although capitalists, to exist, require workers. Hence the standpoint of the working class provides the only possible basis in a capitalist society for a science of values, since its goals and interests, its needs and desires, guided as they are by the neces-

[3] *New York Times,* May 18, 1941. Report of an address at a service commemorating the fiftieth anniversary of Pope Leo XIII's encyclical, "The Condition of the Workingman."

sity for abolishing all exploitation, are *rational* in Spinoza's sense, and thus involve no internal contradiction.

Another way of putting the case is that the use of science in determining values implies or requires a community of interest. In a world where there is no community either science must take a standpoint that aims at attaining community (which involves the recognition of existing conflicts or hostility of interests), or it is doomed to be a pseudo-science that closes its eyes to the most salient facts of the very world it is supposed to deal with empirically. Such is the status of much liberal thought today, which lays claim to a *scientific* approach to social problems. Deweyan pragmatism provides a perfect illustration. Closing its eyes to class conflicts and even to contradictions existing among great capitalist concerns and the imperialist states themselves, this pragmatism sets up as ideals collective bargaining, a League of Nations, and in general the principle of mediation in all possible disputes. But mediation implies in the long run a community of interest, and the Deweyan ideal of sitting around the conference table generally results in a form of compulsory arbitration, where the instrument of compulsion is not rational determination but the strongest force among the opposed parties. One fears that the goal this method aims at and achieves is represented in international affairs by Munich and appeasement rather than by collective action against the aggressor.

Any science that lays claim to dealing with social problems in our society without recognizing the existing objective contradiction of interests is in the paradoxical position of claiming to be knowledge that ignores the central features of the thing known. Without overlooking the limited and partial possibilities for good inherent in a League of Nations or in the conference table in industrial disputes, one must remember that the causes of war between nations and of industrial warfare under capitalism must themselves be scientifically known and then eliminated. And such a decisive result may require something quite different from "mediating" the various presented claims. Science can show the way to peace and prosperity only by recognizing the contradictions in the world in which it must operate and by taking the historically dictated standpoint of that class whose interests are alone in harmony with scientifically feasible objectives.

The realization of a thoroughgoing and complete science of values is, however, a practical task as well as a theoretical objective. While it is now possible, ultimately it requires the creation of a society in which the goals of all are rational, and hence, in Spinoza's terms, harmonious. Then it will be possible scientifically to determine just what all men's needs are, the relations of these to their desires, and how they may be realized. As long as the needs of one class, group, or nation conflict with those of others, science must take sides with those classes and groups whose needs are harmonious with, and require the fuller development of, our productive forces, as is clearly the case today between the democratic states and the Axis powers. Only when such conflicts are eliminated can there be a true and pure "method of intelligence," or scientific method, for the determination of human values and the solution of human problems.

To work for this, then, is the task of science today in the very interest of scientific method and knowledge itself. For any other course leads to obscurantism and scientific reaction. The truly intelligent method is not to try to reconcile the irreconcilable, but to take the standpoint necessary to eliminate conflicts from human social life. The moralist must be scientific today, and the scientist partisan. Only thus can a rational human society be achieved — the ideal of all the great moralists in history.

*　*　*

Great things are not easily attained and men must be continually aware of the danger of judging forces, movements, institutions, and acts in terms of their own smug comforts or loyalties, clothed in highsounding moral phrases, rather than in terms of the highest moral good, freedom. This is the error of such contemporaries as John Dewey and Aldous Huxley, who oppose the only genuine movement towards socialism today on the ground that the means determine the end, and since the necessary means are not satisfactory to them, they remain content with the capitalist world with its poverty, unemployment, and aggressive wars. They ignore, for one thing, that the means necessary for the attainment of socialism are determined far less by the nature of socialism than they are by the nature of capitalism. And this is equally true of every great progressive movement. It is not the *new,* not *that which is yet to be,* that determines the means to be employed, so much as the *old, that which is.* It was not freedom from chattel slavery that determined the *means* the Abolitionists employed, but the nature of the slave-owning power, as Thoreau saw when he wrote that opponents of resistance to the slave power think that the remedy would be worse than the evil. "But," he replied, "it is the fault of the government itself that the

remedy *is* worse than the evil. *It* makes it worse."[4] Similarly, it is the nature of capitalism and not the nature of socialism that determines the means required for its attainment.

Behind this whole means-end controversy stands the great but pathetic Immanuel Kant, whose categorical imperative becomes: "I will be good, no matter the cost to others," and which today degenerates into: "I sincerely believe in a better world but I cannot condone the means used to attain it." It should be plain that this is equivalent to saying that there are two different sources or foundations of the good, one of the good as a means and the other as an end. This does not mean that socialists repudiate the basic moral principles of the human race. They affirm them and follow them. They seek a society in which the great moral principles of the ages may effectively operate, but they refuse to accept any ethical system that places general principles such as "Thou shalt not steal," "Thou shalt not kill," above the welfare of human beings living in society. The Soviets, for example, in collectivizing agriculture, had to sacrifice a good deal, and many people suffered great privations as a result of the tremendous movement for collectivization. This was sad and tragic, but it is little to pay for the prize of no more famines, no more hunger for nearly two hundred millions of people; it is little to pay for the acknowledged solution of one of the modern world's most horrible problems and evils — famine amidst potential plenty. And what in fact was the alternative? The whole future of civilization will acknowledge its debt to the Soviet collectivization program which both enabled the

4 Henry David Thoreau, "Civil Disobedience," in *Walden and Other Writings,* p. 644.

U.S.S.R. to produce agricultural products more abundantly for its civilian and military needs and made possible the "scorched earth" policy and the vast guerrilla warfare against the Nazi invaders. What the Dewey school of moralists teaches is equivalent to saying: "Collectivization of agriculture would be a wonderful thing, providing all with abundance of foodstuffs, eliminating poverty from the countryside, raising immeasurably the cultural level of the farmers. But — the wealthy peasants will resist; they will sabotage; force may have to be used; therefore, we must forego the good of collectivization." And they say precisely this about any movement towards socialism, simply because they apply one set of standards to the ends desired, and another to the means necessary to attain them. Such, too, is the vicious dilemma of those who at least profess to desire a democratic victory over fascism and the maintenance of a free America but who do not wish it so long as the Soviet Union is an ally. Rather defeat, is their slogan, than victory by such means!

This analysis brings us to such questions as those of bourgeois democracy as opposed to proletarian democracy, economic freedom in Herbert Hoover's sense of individual ownership of the means of production versus regulation of all economic relations by the people's power. Or again, similar moral issues are involved if it is a question of individual power at whatever social level versus completely collective decisions, or if it is the question of free speech for fascists in a democracy or free advocacy of capitalism in a socialist society. Under what circumstances, on what moral grounds, may complete democratic rights of individuals or groups be denied or curtailed? Is the democratic process so sacred that it must always be maintained, even under conditions that are certain to bring its downfall? Is it such a thing, as some contemporaries insist, as can never survive the slightest limitation, and hence is "damned if it does, and damned if it doesn't" resist its enemies?

These are certainly some of the most perplexing and debated questions of our time. Most of the difficulties, however, arise from the same confusion over means and ends analyzed above. Has political democracy contributed to human freedom in the sense defined? Immeasurably! Is it an end in itself? Clearly not, if freedom as the dynamic process of realizing human good is the only end in itself. But this does not mean that it is a mere means. It is good in so far as it advances freedom, which it always does unless it is paralyzed by formalisms and abstractions which serve not the interests of the people but those of a dominant minority.

Political democracy must here be distinguished as a living reality, as the instrumentality for the expression and execution of the people's needs and interests, from the fetishism of mere forms which may or may not serve this end. In short, there are both the substance of democracy and its forms, and the latter must necessarily change with changing conditions if the former is to be maintained. Democratic processes are in general a feature of increasing freedom, and their sole test is the extent to which they function in giving freedom. They are not a mere means to something else, for they are a feature of the good or end itself.

On the other hand, they are not the whole good but, in the long run, an inseparable feature of any good society. There is great danger inherent in making political democracy either an end or a means alone, for insoluble problems arise from either. There could have been de-mocracy in Spain today, and possibly no world war taking place, had the working class parties of Spain and the leaders of the Republic been more concerned with the extension of the substance of democ-racy than with some of its traditional forms, and had thus cleaned out from all economic, political, and military control the hostile elements of the land-owning and aristocratic classes. Of course, there would have been a terrific outcry that this is not democracy but dictatorship, but a few million lives might have been saved, and democracy might have been secure in the world today.

Economic freedom must be examined similarly in terms of its actual content at any given time, in terms of its function and the direction it is moving. Taken in the sense of each person doing as he pleases economically, it was once a tre-mendous progressive force. Today under capitalism not only is it a misnomer, for a small group of finance capitalists domi-nate the scene, but appeals to it are re-actionary. In the construction of a social-ist economy there is new economic free-dom, in a higher sense, of a people, led by the organized workers, freeing their economy from the fetters of capitalist control and making it amenable to the needs and rational requirements of the whole society. And this in turn gives way to economic freedom in the still higher sense of an economy actually functioning freely and consciously for the highest good of all. At each level, economic free-dom has specific meanings in terms of what the freedom is free *of* and what it is free *for*, and only dismal confusion arises from the failure to make such distinctions.

Finally, it follows from this dynamic conception of freedom that it can never be diminished by any measures that in-crease the people's power and enable

them the better to control the political, economic, and cultural features of their life. Thus the rule of the majority of people, following the lead of the organ-ized workers, having for its aim the socialist reconstruction of society is no more a step backward in the way of free-dom than was the American disfranchise-ment of slave-owners and of those who bore arms against the government during the reconstruction period following the Civil War. On the contrary, the latter action was an attempt, partly abortive because of the conflicts of interests on the Northern side, to bring about a democratic reconstruction of the South. Exactly the same was true during the period of the American Revolution, when tories had their property confiscated and were deprived of all political rights. The point is that such transition periods are not steps backward from freedom simply because they restrict certain rights and put obstacles in the way of certain groups, but are great steps forward, rep-resenting new, though temporary, forms of the people's growing freedom. This position is in no way to be confused with the "success" or "workability" criteria of American pragmatism, for the simple rea-son that pragmatism has forsaken and denied any long-range conception of freedom or good by which success or failure may be judged.

Lincoln's observations on liberty are as significant today as when they were first uttered. There can be no agreement on what liberty is so long as society is di-vided into different classes with conflict-ing interests. The opposed conceptions of freedom arise out of this very conflict of interests, Lincoln shrewdly observed, and the people once again will repudiate the definition in the wolf's dictionary. Driven partly by necessity that is blind, and increasingly by the necessity that is the product of understanding, men will strive for a better life, for a more rational society, for economic equality and hence for the social ownership of the means of production. This is the struggle for free-dom, under the conditions of our day and age. And this struggle itself is moral or right because freedom is the highest good and that alone by which all acts and institutions can be judged.

Sidney Hook: JOHN DEWEY AND HIS CRITICS

SIR: It is easy to damn absolutes. It is hard, however, to keep them out of one's criticism. Recent discussion of John Dewey's philosophy is a case in point. Not even Dewey's style, that scapegoat of impatient readers, can explain why avowedly liberal American critics in evaluating his thought relapse into posi-tions they have pretended earlier to abandon. Whether one pins on Dewey Mr. Mumford's tag of "pragmatic ac-quiescence," or with Waldo Frank cries shrilly against "prostrate pragmatism," or in cold malice refers to him, à la Stol-berg, as the unconscious ideological rep-resentative of big-business culture — the same confusion is involved. All of his literary critics demand from Dewey what on any theory but an absolutist one they cannot have: viz., a system of values independent of the context and move-ment of the social scene. Because Dewey refuses to condemn our highly indus-trialized technique on the ground that it may some day find an ideal fulfilment in a socialized culture, he is charged with accepting the *status quo* and bowing to the current cults of mechanism, quantity and conformity.

What is involved here is not a mis-understanding of Dewey's politics, but a misunderstanding of his central ethical doctrine — the continuity of ends and means. The doctrine may be rejected but it is first to be understood.

Common-sense moralists as well as many sophisticated theories of criticism introduce a sharp divorce between the end of action and the means used to attain it; between the goal of a move-ment and the methods of getting there; between the principles of valid thought and the specific procedures which illus-trate the principle. It is this assumption which is behind the oft-repeated charge that Dewey is guilty of a deep confusion between ends and means. He tries to tell us what to do without telling us why we should do it. He exhorts us to move without giving us a goal to guide and check our movements. He urges us ever up and onward without tell us what is up or down. Consequently Dewey has no genuine educational goals, he has only a methodology; no theory of the good but only a technique of muddling along; no logic but only a psychology. So the critics!

Let us look a little closer at their position.

Whoever makes a sharp separation be-tween ends and means must face the fol-lowing difficulty: "How are ends, ideals, and principles themselves to be tested?"

Reprinted by permission from the *New Republic*, LXVII, No. 861 (June 3, 1931), 73–74.

Once we grant that the ends are valid, they become as easy to apply as a ruler or a yardstick. And as irrelevant to the moral life! Any length can serve as the measure of distance, but not every end can serve as the measure of a good life. Clearly, if ends are above criticism, all ends are on the same level; the "better" end can only mean the stronger "impulse." Ethics then becomes a part of descriptive psychology, a catalogue of human desires and a study of the conditions under which they arise. If there is any such thing, then, as moral conduct, ends cannot be taken as self-certifying, but must be subject to criticism.

There are two generic ways in which ends may be criticized. We may say either that they are justified by a higher "intuition" or that they are empirically verified in action. It is easy to show that in view of conflicting intuitions of what is higher, the first position leads to arbitrary subjectivism in theory, a theory which often finds a cynical correction in a "might makes right" morality in practice. But what about the second position, Dewey's own? Does it fare any better? How are ends to be tested in action except by applying other ends, themselves taken as final? Dewey's answer is that we never really know what our ends are before we have reflected upon the probable consequences of carrying them out in practice. He holds that the only way to criticize our ends is to ask what results from the use of the means designed to realize those ends. For Dewey, wherever action is intelligent and responsible, the means are a part of the ends. We do not know what we have chosen unless we see what is involved in bringing that choice about; we cannot proclaim allegiance to exalted ideals as if that freed us from the moral imperative of judging them by their consequences.

But still, one asks, aren't there certain standards which we must use in order to determine whether the consequences of acting on our ends, of finding the specific means, are satisfactory? Certainly there are — a whole host of them, like friendship, wisdom, beauty, courage, health, security, adventure. But note. Although they are immediate goods none of them is finally good. None is supreme, none above the necessity of pointing to consequent goods in case its own immediate quality is threatened. For it is only too clear that the ethical and material goods of this world are not necessarily in harmony with each other. One good conflicts with another: knowledge with happiness; serenity with intensity. In no two situations can we resolve the conflict in exactly the same way. Hence, although we use these goods as principles to guide us in our ways, they never can determine the unique good of the particular situation. True, they are involved in every specific case. But there is something more always present which controls the manner and extent of their operation.

Ethical standards function like scientific hypotheses. They guide conduct but are controlled by what they lead us to. A morality which flings its "ought" to the world irrespective of what the world at any moment "is," which refuses to have its ends rough-hewn by the critical test of experimental living, converts personal caprice or dead tradition into immutable first principles. For Dewey moral ends are ends chosen after reflection, chosen with a full consciousness of what we want, of how to get it and of what we must give up for it. Intelligence and sincerity are central to the good life. To know is not enough. To know by doing is all there is to genuinely reflective morality.

Observe now how the literary critics of Dewey understand him. Where

Dewey writes that there are no standards or goods above criticism, they read him as if he denied the existence or necessity of *any* standards. Where he insists that ideals must have a natural basis in the social order, they hear him say in substance: "Whatever is, is right." Where Dewey says "Don't be too sure about your goal unless it can guide you a little way ahead so that you can take another reading," they complain, "Dewey tells us how to get ten steps ahead, but he does not tell us where and what the goal is." Where Dewey affirms that science and technology are here to stay, that they can and should be the basis of a new social order, he is accused of surrendering to the drift of mechanical forces. And,

finally, when Dewey refuses to give the blueprints of the cultural pattern he expects the new social order to evolve, his critics exclaim that he does not know what he wants.

It is the failure to come to grips with the experimental theory of knowledge and morals which makes these criticisms of Dewey's social philosophy seem so pathetically utopian.

Dewey's idea is a socialized America. In terms of his own position, the only quarrel one can have with him is his failure to appreciate the instrumental value of *class struggle* rather than class collaboration in effecting the transition from Corporate America to Collective America.

John Dewey:

LIBERALISM AND SOCIAL ACTION

NOTHING is blinder than the supposition that we live in a society and world so static that either nothing new will happen or else it will happen because of the use of violence. Social change is here as a fact, a fact having multifarious forms and marked in intensity. Changes that are revolutionary in effect are in process in every phase of life. Transformations in the family, the church, the school, in science and art, in economic and political relations, are occurring so swiftly that imagination is baffled in attempt to lay hold of them. Flux does not have to be created. But it does have to be directed. It has to be so

controlled that it will move to some end in accordance with the principles of life, since life itself is development. Liberalism is committed to an end that is at once enduring and flexible: the liberation of individuals so that realization of their capacities may be the law of their life. It is committed to the use of freed intelligence as the method of directing change. In any case, civilization is faced with the problem of uniting the changes that are going on into a coherent pattern of social organization. The liberal spirit is marked by its own picture of the pattern that is required: a social organization that will make possible effective liberty and opportunity for personal growth in mind and spirit in all individuals. Its present need is recognition that established material security is a prerequisite of the ends which it cherishes, so that, the basis of life being secure, individuals may actively share in the wealth of cultural resources that now exist and may contribute, each in his own way, to their further enrichment.

The fact of change has been so continual and so intense that it overwhelms our minds. We are bewildered by the spectacle of its rapidity, scope and intensity. It is not surprising that men have protected themselves from the impact of such vast change by resorting to what psycho-analysis has taught us to call rationalizations, in other words, protective fantasies. The Victorian idea that change is a part of an evolution that necessarily leads through successive stages to some preordained divine far-off event is one rationalization. The conception of a sudden, complete, almost catastrophic, transformation, to be brought about by the victory of the proletariat over the class now dominant, is a similar rationalization. But men have met the impact of change in the realm of actuality, mostly by drift and by temporary, usually incoherent, improvisations. Liberalism, like every other theory of life, has suffered from the state of confused uncertainty that is the lot of a world suffering from rapid and varied change for which there is no intellectual and moral preparation.

Because of this lack of mental and moral preparation the impact of swiftly moving changes produced, as I have just said, confusion, uncertainty and drift. Change in patterns of belief, desire and purpose has lagged behind the modification of the external conditions under which men associate. Industrial habits have changed most rapidly; there has followed at considerable distance, change in political relations; alterations in legal relations and methods have lagged even more, while changes in the institutions that deal most directly with patterns of thought and belief have taken place to the least extent. This fact defines the primary, though not by any means the ultimate, responsibility of a liberalism that intends to be a vital force. Its work is first of all education, in the broadest sense of that term. Schooling is a part of the work of education, but education in its full meaning includes all the influences that go to form the attitudes and dispositions (of desire as well as of belief), which constitute dominant habits of mind and character.

Let me mention three changes that have taken place in one of the institutions in which immense shifts have occurred, but that are still relatively external — external in the sense that the pattern of intelligent purpose and emotion has not been correspondingly modified. Civilization existed for most of human history in a state of scarcity in the material basis for a humane life. Our ways of thinking, planning and working have been attuned to this fact. Thanks to science and technology we now live in an age of potential plenty. The immediate effect of the emergence of the new possibility was simply to stimulate, to a point of incredible exaggeration, the striving for the material resources, called wealth, opened to men in the new vista. It is a characteristic of all development, physiological and mental, that when a new force and factor appears, it is first pushed to an extreme. Only when its possibilities have been exhausted (at least relatively) does it take its place in the life perspective. The economic-material phase of life, which belongs in the basal ganglia of society, has usurped for more than a century the cortex of the social body. The habits of desire and effort that were bred in the age of scarcity do not readily subordinate themselves and take the place of the matter-of-course routine that becomes appropriate to them when machines and impersonal power have the capacity to liberate man from bondage to the strivings that were once needed to make secure his physical basis. Even now when there is a vision of an age of abundance and when the vision is supported by hard fact, it is material security as an end that appeals to most rather than the way of living which this security makes possible. Men's minds are still pathetically held in the clutch of old habits and haunted by old memories.

For, in the second place, insecurity is the natural child and the foster child, too, of scarcity. Early liberalism emphasized the importance of insecurity as a fundamentally necessary economic motive, holding that without this goad men would not work, abstain or accumulate. Formulation of this conception was new. But the fact that was formulated was nothing new. It was deeply rooted in the habits that were formed in the long struggle against material scarcity. The system that goes by the name of capitalism is a systematic manifestation of desires and purposes built up in an age of ever threatening want and now carried over into a time of ever increasing potential plenty. The conditions that generate insecurity for the many no longer spring from nature. They are found in institutions and arrangements that are within deliberate human control. Surely this change marks one of the greatest revolutions that has taken place in all human history. Because of it, insecurity is not now the motive to work and sacrifice but to despair. It is not an instigation to put forth energy but to an impotency that

can be converted from death into endurance only by charity. But the habits of mind and action that modify institutions to make potential abundance an actuality are still so inchoate that most of us discuss labels like individualism, socialism and communism instead of even perceiving the possibility, much less the necessity for realizing what can and should be.

In the third place, the patterns of belief and purpose that still dominate economic institutions were formed when individuals produced with their hands, alone or in small groups. The notion that society in general is served by the unplanned coincidence of the consequences of a vast multitude of efforts put forth by isolated individuals without reference to any social end, was also something new as a formulation. But it also formulated the working principle of an epoch which the advent of new forces of production was to bring to an end. It demands no great power of intelligence to see that under present conditions the isolated individual is well-nigh helpless. Concentration and corporate organization are the rule. But the concentration and corporate organization are still controlled in their operation by ideas that were institutionalized in eons of separate individual effort. The attempts at coöperation for mutual benefit that are put forth are precious as experimental moves. But that society itself should see to it that a coöperative industrial order be instituted, one that is consonant with the realities of production enforced by an era of machinery and power, is so novel an idea to the general mind that its mere suggestion is hailed with abusive epithets — sometimes with imprisonment.

When, then, I say that the first object of a renascent liberalism is education, I mean that its task is to aid in producing the habits of mind and character, the intellectual and moral patterns, that are somewhere near even with the actual movements of events. It is, I repeat, the split between the latter as they have externally occurred and the ways of desiring, thinking, and of putting emotion and purpose into execution that is the basic cause of present confusion in mind and paralysis in action. The educational task cannot be accomplished merely by working upon men's minds, without action that effects actual change in institutions. The idea that dispositions and attitudes can be altered by merely "moral" means conceived of as something that goes on wholly inside of persons is itself one of the old patterns that has to be changed. Thought, desire and purpose exist in a constant give and take of interaction with environing conditions. But resolute thought is the first step in that change of action that will itself carry further the needed change in patterns of mind and character.

In short, liberalism must now become radical, meaning by "radical" perception of the necessity of thoroughgoing changes in the set-up of institutions and corresponding activity to bring the changes to pass. For the gulf between what the actual situation makes possible and the actual state itself is so great that it cannot be bridged by piecemeal policies undertaken *ad hoc*. The process of producing the changes will be, in any case, a gradual one. But "reforms" that deal now with this abuse and now with that without having a social goal based upon an inclusive plan, differ entirely from effort at re-forming, in its literal sense, the institutional scheme of things. The liberals of more than a century ago were denounced in their time as subversive radicals, and only when the new economic order was established did they become

apologists for the *status quo* or else content with social patchwork. If radicalism be defined as perception of need for radical change, then today any liberalism which is not also radicalism is irrelevant and doomed.

But radicalism also means, in the minds of many, both supporters and opponents, dependence upon use of violence as the main method of effecting drastic changes. Here the liberal parts company. For he is committed to the organization of intelligent action as the chief method. Any frank discussion of the issue must recognize the extent to which those who decry the use of any violence are themselves willing to resort to violence and are ready to put their will into operation. Their fundamental objection is to change in the economic institution that now exists, and for its maintenance they resort to the use of the force that is placed in their hands by this very institution. They do not need to advocate the use of force; their only need is to employ it. Force, rather than intelligence, is built into the procedures of the existing social system, regularly as coercion, in times of crisis as overt violence. The legal system, conspicuously in its penal aspect, more subtly in civil practice, rests upon coercion. Wars are the methods recurrently used in settlement of disputes between nations. One school of radicals dwells upon the fact that in the past the transfer of power in one society has either been accomplished by or attended with violence. But what we need to realize is that physical force is used, at least in the form of coercion, in the very set-up of our society. That the competitive system, which was thought of by early liberals as the means by which the latent abilities of individuals were to be evoked and directed into socially useful channels, is now in fact a state of scarcely disguised battle hardly needs to be dwelt upon. That the control of the means of production by the few in legal possession operates as a standing agency of coercion of the many, may need emphasis in statement, but is surely evident to one who is willing to observe and honestly report the existing scene. It is foolish to regard the political state as the only agency now endowed with coercive power. Its exercise of this power is pale in contrast with that exercised by concentrated and organized property interests.

It is not surprising in view of our standing dependence upon the use of coercive force that at every time of crisis coercion breaks out into open violence. In this country, with its tradition of violence fostered by frontier conditions and by the conditions under which immigration went on during the greater part of our history, resort to violence is especially recurrent on the part of those who are in power. In times of imminent change, our verbal and sentimental worship of the Constitution, with its guarantees of civil liberties of expression, publication and assemblage, readily goes overboard. Often the officials of the law are the worst offenders, acting as agents of some power that rules the economic life of a community. What is said about the value of free speech as a safety valve is then forgotten with the utmost of ease: a comment, perhaps, upon the weakness of the defense of freedom of expression that values it simply as a means of blowing-off steam.

It is not pleasant to face the extent to which, as matter of fact, coercive and violent force is relied upon in the present social system as a means of social control. It is much more agreeable to evade the fact. But unless the fact is acknowledged as a fact in its full depth and breadth, the meaning of dependence upon intelli-

gence as the alternative method of social direction will not be grasped. Failure in acknowledgment signifies, among other things, failure to realize that those who propagate the dogma of dependence upon force have the sanction of much that is already entrenched in the existing system. They would but turn the use of it to opposite ends. The assumption that the method of intelligence already rules and that those who urge the use of violence are introducing a new element into the social picture may not be hypocritical but it is unintelligently unaware of what is actually involved in intelligence as an alternative method of social action.

I begin with an example of what is really involved in the issue. Why is it, apart from our tradition of violence, that liberty of expression is tolerated and even lauded when social affairs seem to be going in a quiet fashion, and yet is so readily destroyed whenever matters grow critical? The general answer, of course, is that at bottom social institutions have habituated us to the use of force in some veiled form. But a part of the answer is found in our ingrained habit of regarding intelligence as an individual possession and its exercise as an individual right. It is false that freedom of inquiry and of expression are not modes of action. They are exceedingly potent modes of action. The reactionary grasps this fact, in practice if not in express idea, more quickly than the liberal, who is too much given to holding that this freedom is innocent of consequences, as well as being a merely individual right. The result is that this liberty is tolerated as long as it does not seem to menace in any way the *status quo* of society. When it does, every effort is put forth to identify the established order with the public good. When this identification is established, it follows that any merely individual right must yield to the general welfare. As long as freedom of thought and speech is claimed as a merely individual right, it will give way, as do other merely personal claims, when it is, or is successfully represented to be, in opposition to the general welfare.

I would not in the least disparage the noble fight waged by early liberals in behalf of individual freedom of thought and expression. We owe more to them than it is possible to record in words. No more eloquent words have ever come from any one than those of Justice Brandeis in the case of a legislative act that in fact restrained freedom of political expression. He said: "Those who won our independence believed that the final end of the State was to make men free to develop their faculties, and that in its government the deliberative faculties should prevail over the arbitrary. They valued liberty both as an end and as a means. They believed liberty to be the secret of happiness and courage to be the secret of liberty. They believed that freedom to think as you will and to speak as you think are means indispensable to the discovery and spread of political truth; that without free speech and assembly discussion would be futile; that with them, discussion affords ordinarily adequate protection against the dissemination of noxious doctrines; that the greatest menace to freedom is an inert people; that public discussion is a political duty; and that this should be a fundamental principle of the American government." This is the creed of a fighting liberalism. But the issue I am raising is connected with the fact that these words are found in a dissenting, a minority opinion of the Supreme Court of the United States. The public function of free individual thought and speech is clearly recognized in the words quoted. But the reception of

the truth of the words is met by an obstacle: the old habit of defending liberty of thought and expression as something inhering in individuals apart from and even in opposition to social claims.

Liberalism has to assume the responsibility for making it clear that intelligence is a social asset and is clothed with a function as public as is its origin, in the concrete, in social coöperation. It was Comte who, in reaction against the purely individualistic ideas that seemed to him to underlie the French Revolution, said that in mathematics, physics and astronomy there is no right of private conscience. If we remove the statement from the context of actual scientific procedure, it is dangerous because it is false. The individual inquirer has not only the right but the duty to criticize the ideas, theories and "laws" that are current in science. But if we take the statement in the context of scientific method, it indicates that he carries on this criticism in virtue of a socially generated body of knowledge and by means of methods that are not of private origin and possession. He uses a method that retains public validity even when innovations are introduced in its use and application.

Henry George, speaking of ships that ply the ocean with a velocity of five or six hundred miles a day, remarked, "There is nothing whatever to show that the men who today build and navigate and use such ships are one whit superior in any physical or mental quality to their ancestors, whose best vessel was a coracle of wicker and hide. The enormous improvement which these ships show is not an improvement of human nature; it is an improvement of society — it is due to a wider and fuller union of individual efforts in accomplishment of common ends." This single instance, duly pondered, gives a better idea of the nature of intelligence and its social office than would a volume of abstract dissertation. Consider merely two of the factors that enter in and their social consequences. Consider what is involved in the production of steel, from the first use of fire and then the crude smelting of ore, to the processes that now effect the mass production of steel. Consider also the development of the power of guiding ships across trackless wastes from the day when they hugged the shore, steering by visible sun and stars, to the appliances that now enable a sure course to be taken. It would require a heavy tome to describe the advances in science, in mathematics, astronomy, physics, chemistry, that have made these two things possible. The record would be an account of a vast multitude of coöperative efforts, in which one individual uses the results provided for him by a countless number of other individuals, and uses them so as to add to the common and public store. A survey of such facts brings home the actual social character of intelligence as it actually develops and makes its way. Survey of the consequences upon the ways of living of individuals and upon the terms on which men associate together, due to the new method of transportation would take us to the wheat farmer of the prairies, the cattle raiser of the plains, the cotton grower of the South; into a multitude of mills and factories, and to the counting-room of banks, and what would be seen in this country would be repeated in every country of the globe.

It is to such things as these, rather than to abstract and formal psychology that we must go if we would learn the nature of intelligence: in itself, in its origin and development, and its uses and consequences. At this point, I should like to recur to an idea put forward in the preceding chapter. I then referred to the contempt often expressed for reliance upon intelligence as a social method, and I said this scorn is due to the identification of intelligence with native endowments of individuals. In contrast to this notion, I spoke of the power of individuals to appropriate and respond to the intelligence, the knowledge, ideas and purposes that have been integrated in the medium in which individuals live. Each of us knows, for example, some mechanic of ordinary native capacity who is intelligent within the matters of his calling. He has lived in an environment in which the cumulative intelligence of a multitude of coöperating individuals is embodied, and by the use of his native capacities he makes some phase of this intelligence his own. Given a social medium in whose institutions the available knowledge, ideas and art of humanity were incarnate, and the average individual would rise to undreamed heights of social and political intelligence.

The rub, the problem is found in the proviso. Can the intelligence actually existent and potentially available be embodied in that institutional medium in which an individual thinks, desires and acts? Before dealing directly with this question, I wish to say something about the operation of intelligence in our present political institutions, as exemplified by current practices of democratic government. I would not minimize the advance scored in substitution of methods of discussion and conference for the method of arbitrary rule. But the better is too often the enemy of the still better. Discussion, as the manifestation of intelligence in political life, stimulates publicity; by its means sore spots are brought to light that would otherwise remain hidden. It affords opportunity for promulgation of new ideas. Compared with despotic rule, it is an invitation to individuals to concern themselves with public affairs. But discussion and dialectic, however indispensable they are to the elaboration of ideas and policies after ideas are once put forth, are weak reeds to depend upon for systematic origination of comprehensive plans, the plans that are required if the problem of social organization is to be met. There was a time when discussion, the comparison of ideas already current so as to purify and clarify them, was thought to be sufficient in discovery of the structure and laws of physical nature. In the latter field, the method was displaced by that of experimental observation guided by comprehensive working hypotheses, and using all the resources made available by mathematics.

But we still depend upon the method of discussion, with only incidental scientific control, in politics. Our system of popular suffrage, immensely valuable as it is in comparison with what preceded it, exhibits the idea that intelligence is an individualistic possession, at best enlarged by public discussion. Existing political practice, with its complete ignoring of occupational groups and the organized knowledge and purposes that are involved in the existence of such groups, manifests a dependence upon a summation of individuals quantitatively, similar to Bentham's purely quantitative formula of the greatest sum of pleasures of the greatest possible number. The formation of parties or, as the eighteenth-century writers called them, factions, and the system of party government is the practically necessary counterweight to a numerical and atomistic individualism. The idea that the conflict of parties will, by means of public discussion, bring out necessary public truths is a kind of political watered-down version of the Hegelian dialectic, with its synthesis arrived at by a union of antithetical conceptions. The method has nothing in common with the procedure of organized coöperative inquiry which has won the triumphs of science in the field of physical nature.

Intelligence in politics when it is identified with discussion means reliance upon symbols. The invention of language is probably the greatest single invention achieved by humanity. The development of political forms that promote the use of symbols in place of arbitrary power was another great invention. The nineteenth-century establishment of parliamentary institutions, written constitutions and the suffrage as means of political rule, is a tribute to the power of symbols. But symbols are significant only in connection with realities behind them. No intelligent observer can deny, I think, that they are often used in party politics as a substitute for realities instead of as means of contact with them. Popular literacy, in connection with the telegraph, cheap postage and the printing press, has enormously multiplied the number of those influenced. That which we term education has done a good deal to generate habits that put symbols in the place of realities. The forms of popular government make necessary the elaborate use of words to influence political action. "Propaganda" is the inevitable consequence of the combination of these influences and it extends to every area of life. Words not only take the place of realities but are themselves debauched. Decline in the prestige of suffrage and of parliamentary government are intimately associated with the belief, manifest in practice even if not expressed in words, that intelligence is an individual possession to be reached by means of verbal persuasion.

This fact suggests, by way of contrast, the genuine meaning of intelligence in connection with public opinion, sentiment and action. The crisis in democracy demands the substitution of the intelligence that is exemplified in scientific procedure for the kind of intelligence that is now accepted. The need for this change is not exhausted in the demand for greater honesty and impartiality, even though these qualities be now corrupted by discussion carried on mainly for purposes of party supremacy and for imposition of some special but concealed interest. These qualities need to be restored. But the need goes further. The social use of intelligence would remain deficient even if these moral traits were exalted, and yet intelligence continued to be identified simply with discussion and persuasion, necessary as are these things. Approximation to use of scientific method in investigation and of the engineering mind in the invention and projection of far-reaching social plans is demanded. The habit of considering social realities in terms of cause and effect and social policies in terms of means and consequences is still inchoate. The contrast between the state of intelligence in politics and in the physical control of nature is to be taken literally. What has happened in this latter is the outstanding demonstration of the meaning of organized intelligence. The combined effect of science and technology has released more productive energies in a bare hundred years than stands to the credit of prior human history in its entirety. Productively it has multiplied nine million times in the last generation alone. The prophetic vision of Francis Bacon of subjugation of the energies of nature through change in methods of inquiry has wellnigh been realized. The stationary engine, the locomotive, the dynamo, the motor car, turbine, telegraph, telephone, radio and moving picture are not the products of either isolated individual minds nor of the particular economic régime called capitalism. They are the fruit of methods that first penetrated to the working causalities of nature and then utilized the resulting knowledge in bold imaginative ventures of invention and construction.

We hear a great deal in these days about class conflict. The past history of man is held up to us as almost exclusively a record of struggles between classes, ending in the victory of a class that had been oppressed and the transfer of power to it. It is difficult to avoid reading the past in terms of the contemporary scene. Indeed, fundamentally it is impossible to avoid this course. With a certain proviso, it is highly important that we are compelled to follow this path. For the past as past is gone, save for esthetic enjoyment and refreshment, while the present is with us. Knowledge of the past is significant only as it deepens and extends our understanding of the present. Yet there is a proviso. We must grasp the things that are most important in the present when we turn to the past and not allow ourselves to be misled by secondary phenomena no matter how intense and immediately urgent they are. Viewed from this standpoint, the rise of scientific method and of technology based upon it is the genuinely active force in producing the vast complex of changes the world is now undergoing, not the class struggle whose spirit and method are opposed to science. If we lay hold upon the causal force exercised by this embodiment of intelligence we shall know where to turn for the means of directing further change.

When I say that scientific method and technology have been the active force in producing the revolutionary transformations society is undergoing, I do not imply no other forces have been at work to arrest, deflect and corrupt their operation. Rather this fact is positively implied. At this point, indeed, is located the conflict that underlies the confusions and uncertainties of the present scene. The conflict is between institutions and habits originating in the pre-scientific and pre-technological age and the new forces generated by science and technology. The application of science, to a considerable degree, even its own growth, has been conditioned by the system to which the name of capitalism is given, a rough designation of a complex of political and legal arrangements centering about a particular mode of economic relations. Because of the conditioning of science and technology by this setting, the second and humanly most important part of Bacon's prediction has so far largely missed realization. The conquest of natural energies has not accrued to the betterment of the common human estate in anything like the degree he anticipated.

Because of conditions that were set by the legal institutions and the moral ideas existing when the scientific and industrial revolutions came into being, the chief usufruct of the latter has been appropriated by a relatively small class. Industrial entrepreneurs have reaped out of all proportion to what they sowed. By obtaining private ownership of the means of production and exchange they deflected a considerable share of the results of increased productivity to their private pockets. This appropriation was not the fruit of criminal conspiracy or of sinister intent. It was sanctioned not only by legal institutions of age-long standing but by the entire prevailing moral code. The institution of private property long antedated feudal times. It is the institution with which men have lived, with few exceptions, since the dawn of civilization. Its existence has deeply impressed itself upon mankind's moral conceptions. Moreover, the new industrial forces tended to break down many of the rigid class barriers that had been in force, and to give to millions a new outlook and inspire a new hope; — especially in this country with no feudal background and no fixed class system.

Since the legal institutions and the patterns of mind characteristic of ages of civilization still endure, there exists the conflict that brings confusion into every phase of present life. The problem of bringing into being a new social orientation and organization is, when reduced to its ultimates, the problem of using the new resources of production, made possible by the advance of physical science, for social ends, for what Bentham called the greatest good of the greatest number. Institutional relationships fixed in the pre-scientific age stand in the way of accomplishing this great transformation. Lag in mental and moral patterns provides the bulwark of the older institutions; in expressing the past they still express present beliefs, outlooks and purposes. Here is the place where the problem of liberalism centers today.

The argument drawn from past history that radical change must be effected by means of class struggle, culminating in open war, fails to discriminate between the two forces, one active, the other resistant and deflecting, that have produced the social scene in which we live. The active force is, as I have said, scientific method and technological application. The opposite force is that of older institutions and the habits that have grown up around them. Instead of discrimination between forces and distribution of their consequences, we find the two things lumped together. The compound is labeled the capitalistic or the bourgeois class, and to this class as a class is imputed all the important features of present industrialized society — much as the defenders of the régime of economic liberty exercised for private property are accustomed to attribute every improvement made in the last century and a half to the same capitalistic régime. Thus in orthodox communist literature, from the Communist Manifesto of 1848 to the present day, we are told that the bourgeoisie, the name for a distinctive class, has done this and that. It has, so it is said, given a cosmopolitan character to production and consumption; has destroyed the national basis of industry; has agglomerated population in urban centers; has transferred power from the country to the city, in the process of creating colossal productive force, its chief achievement. In addition, it has created crises of ever renewed intensity; has created imperialism of a new type in frantic effort to control raw materials and markets. Finally, it has created a new class, the proletariat, and has created it as a class having a common interest opposed to that of the bourgeoisie, and is giving an irresistible stimulus to its organization, first as a class and then as a political power. According to the economic version of the Hegelian dialectic, the bourgeois class is thus creating its own complete and polar opposite, and this in time will end the old power and rule. The class struggle of veiled civil war will finally burst into open revolution and the result will be either the common ruin of the contending parties or a revolutionary reconstitution of society at large through a transfer of power from one class to another.

The position thus sketched unites vast sweep with great simplicity. I am concerned with it here only as far as it emphasizes the idea of a struggle between classes, culminating in open and violent warfare as being the method for production of radical social change. For, be it noted, the issue is not whether some amount of violence will accompany the effectuation of radical change of institutions. The question is whether force or intelligence is to be the method upon which we consistently rely and to whose promotion we devote our energies. Insistence that the use of violent force is *inevitable* limits the use of available intelligence, for wherever the inevitable reigns intelligence cannot be used. Commitment to inevitability is always the fruit of dogma; intelligence does not pretend to *know* save as a result of experimentation, the opposite of preconceived dogma. Moreover, acceptance in advance of the inevitability of violence tends to produce the use of violence in cases where peaceful methods might otherwise avail. The curious fact is that while it is generally admitted that this and that particular social problem, say of the family, or railroads or banking, must be solved, if at all, by the method of intelligence, yet there is supposed to be some one all-inclusive social problem which can be solved only by the use of violence. This fact would be inexplicable were it not a conclusion from dogma as its premise.

It is frequently asserted that the method of experimental intelligence can be applied to physical facts because physical nature does not present conflicts of class interests, while it is inapplicable to society because the latter is so deeply marked by incompatible interests. It is then assumed that the "experimentalist" is one who has chosen to ignore the uncomfortable fact of conflicting interests. Of course, there *are* conflicting interests; otherwise there would be no social problems. The problem under discussion is precisely *how* conflicting claims are to be settled in the interest of the widest possible contribution to the interests of all — or at least of the great majority. The method of democracy — inasfar as it is that of organized intelligence — is to bring these conflicts out into the open where their special claims can be seen and appraised, where they can be discussed and judged in the light of more inclusive interests than are represented by either of them separately. There is, for example, a clash of interests between munition manufacturers and most of the rest of the population. The more the respective claims of the two are publicly and scientifically weighed, the more likely it is that the public interest will be disclosed and be made effective. There is an undoubted objective clash of interests between finance-capitalism that controls the means of production and whose profit is served by maintaining relative scarcity, and idle workers and hungry consumers. But what generates violent strife is failure to bring the conflict into the light of intelligence where the conflicting interests can be adjudicated in behalf of the interest of the great majority. Those most committed to the dogma of inevitable force recognize the need for intelligently discovering and expressing the dominant social interest up to a certain point and then draw back. The "experimentalist" is one who would see to it that the method depended upon by all in some degree in every democratic community be followed through to completion.

In spite of the existence of class conflicts, amounting at times to veiled civil war, any one habituated to the use of the method of science will view with considerable suspicion the erection of actual human beings into fixed entities called classes, having no overlapping interests and so internally unified and externally separated that they are made the protagonists of history — itself hypothetical. Such an idea of classes is a survival of a rigid logic that once prevailed in the sciences of nature, but that no longer has any place there. This conversion of abstractions into entities smells more of a dialectic of concepts than of a realistic examination of facts, even though it makes more of an emotional appeal to many than do the results of the latter. To say that all past historic social progress has been the result of coöperation and not of conflict would be also an exaggeration. But exaggeration against exaggeration, it is the more reasonable of the two. And it is no exaggeration to say that the measure of civilization is the degree in which the method of coöperative intelligence replaces the method of brute conflict.

But the point I am especially concerned with just here is the indiscriminate lumping together as a single force of two different things — the results of scientific technology and of a legal system of property relations. It is science and technology that have had the revolutionary social effect while the legal system has been the relatively static element. According to the Marxians themselves, the economic foundations of society consist of two things, the forces of production on one side and, on the other side, the social relations of production, that is, the legal property system under which the former operates. The latter lags behind, and "revolutions" are produced by the power of the forces of production to change the system of institutional relations. But what are the modern forces of production save those of scientific technology? And what is scientific technology save a large-scale demonstration of organized intelligence in action?

It is quite true that what is happening socially is the result of the combination of the two factors, one dynamic, the other relatively static. If we choose to call the combination by the name of capitalism, then it is true, or a truism, that capitalism is the "cause" of all the important social changes that have occurred — an argument that the representatives of capitalism are eager to put forward whenever the increase of productivity is in question. But if we want to *understand,* and not just to paste labels, unfavorable or favorable as the case may be, we shall certainly begin and end with discrimination. Colossal increase in productivity, the bringing of men together in cities and large factories, the elimination of distance, the accumulation of capital, fixed and liquid — these things would have come about, at a certain stage, no matter what the established institutional system. They are the consequence of the new means of technological production. Certain other things have happened because of inherited institutions and the habits of belief and character that accompany and support them. If we begin at this point, we shall see that the release of productivity is the product of coöperatively organized intelligence, and shall also see that the institutional framework is precisely that which is not subjected as yet, in any considerable measure, to the impact of inventive and constructive intelligence. That coercion and oppression on a large scale exist, no honest person can deny. But these things are not the product of science and technology but of the perpetuation of old institutions and patterns untouched by scientific method. The inference to be drawn is clear.

The argument, drawn from history, that great social changes have been effected only by violent means, needs considerable qualification, in view of the vast scope of changes that are taking place without the use of violence. But even if it be admitted to hold of the past, the conclusion that violence is the method now to be depended upon does not follow — unless one is committed to a dogmatic philosophy of history. The radical who insists that the future method of change must be like that of the past has much in common with the hidebound reactionary who holds to the past as an ultimate fact. Both overlook the *fact that history in being a process of change generates change not only in details but also in the method of directing social change.* I recur to what I said at the beginning of this chapter. It is true that the social order is largely conditioned by the use of coercive force, bursting at times into open violence. But what is also true is that mankind now has in its possession a new method, that of coöperative and experimental science which expresses the method of intelligence. I should be meeting dogmatism with dogmatism if I asserted that the existence of this historically new factor completely invalidates all arguments drawn from the effect of force in the past. But it is within the bounds of reason to assert that the presence of this social factor demands that the present situation be analyzed on its own terms, and not be rigidly subsumed under fixed conceptions drawn from the past.

Any analysis made in terms of the present situation will not fail to note one fact that militates powerfully against arguments drawn from past use of violence. Modern warfare is destructive beyond anything known in older times.

This increased destructiveness is due primarily, of course, to the fact that science has raised to a new pitch of destructive power all the agencies of armed hostility. But it is also due to the much greater interdependence of all the elements of society. The bonds that hold modern communities and states together are as delicate as they are numerous. The self-sufficiency and independence of a local community, characteristic of more primitive societies, have disappeared in every highly industrialized country. The gulf that once separated the civilian population from the military has virtually gone. War involves paralysis of all normal social activities, and not merely the meeting of armed forces in the field. The Communist Manifesto presented two alternatives: *either* the revolutionary change and transfer of power to the proletariat, *or* the common ruin of the contending parties. Today, the civil war that would be adequate to effect transfer of power and a reconstitution of society at large, as understood by official Communists, would seem to present but one possible consequence: the ruin of all parties and the destruction of civilized life. This fact alone is enough to lead us to consider the potentialities of the method of intelligence.

The argument for putting chief dependence upon violence as the method of effecting radical change is, moreover, usually put in a way that proves altogether too much for its own case. It is said that the dominant economic class has all the agencies of power in its hands, directly the army, militia and police; indirectly, the courts, schools, press and radio. I shall not stop to analyze this statement. But if one admits it to be valid, the conclusion to be drawn is surely the folly of resorting to a use of force against force

that is so well intrenched. The positive conclusion that emerges is that conditions that would promise success in the case of use of force are such as to make possible great change without any great recourse to such a method.*

Those who uphold the necessity of dependence upon violence usually much oversimplify the case by setting up a disjunction they regard as self-evident. They say that the sole alternative is putting our trust in parliamentary procedures as they now exist. This isolation of law-making from other social forces and agencies that are constantly operative is wholly unrealistic. Legislatures and congresses do not exist in a vacuum — not even the judges on the bench live in completely secluded sound-proof chambers. The assumption that it is possible for the constitution and activities of law-making bodies to persist unchanged while society itself is undergoing great change is an exercise in verbal formal logic.

It is true that in this country, because of the interpretations made by courts of a written constitution, our political institutions are unusually inflexible. It is also true, as well as even more important (because it is a factor in causing this rigidity) that our institutions, democratic in form, tend to favor in substance a privileged plutocracy. Nevertheless, it is sheer defeatism to assume in advance of actual trial that democratic political institutions are incapable either of further development or of constructive social

* It should be noted that Marx himself was not completely committed to the dogma of the inevitability of force as the means of effecting revolutionary changes in the system of "social relations." For at one time he contemplated that the change might occur in Great Britain and the United States, and possibly in Holland, by peaceful means.

application. Even as they now exist, the forms of representative government are potentially capable of expressing the public will when that assumes anything like unification. And there is nothing inherent in them that forbids their supplementation by political agencies that represent definitely economic social interests, like those of producers and consumers.

The final argument in behalf of the use of intelligence is that as are the means used so are the actual ends achieved — that is, the consequences. I know of no greater fallacy than the claim of those who hold to the dogma of the necessity of brute force that this use will be the method of calling genuine democracy into existence — of which they profess themselves the simon-pure adherents. It requires an unusually credulous faith in the Hegelian dialectic of opposites to think that all of a sudden the use of force by a class will be transmuted into a democratic classless society. Force breeds counterforce; the Newtonian law of action and reaction still holds in physics, and violence is physical. To profess democracy as an ultimate ideal and the suppression of democracy as a means to the ideal may be possible in a country that has never known even rudimentary democracy, but when professed in a country that has anything of a genuine democratic spirit in its traditions, it signifies desire for possession and retention of power by a class, whether that class be called Fascist or Proletarian. In the light of what happens in non-democratic countries, it is pertinent to ask whether the rule of a class signifies the dictatorship of the majority, or dictatorship over the chosen class by a minority party; whether dissenters are allowed even within the class the party claims to represent; and whether the development of

literature and the other arts proceeds according to a formula prescribed by a party in conformity with a doctrinaire dogma of history and of infallible leadership, or whether artists are free from regimentation? Until these questions are satisfactorily answered, it is permissible to look with considerable suspicion upon those who assert that suppression of democracy is the road to the adequate establishment of genuine democracy. The one exception — and that apparent rather than real — to dependence upon organized intelligence as the method for directing social change is found when society through an authorized majority has entered upon the path of social experimentation leading to great social change, and a minority refuses by force to permit the method of intelligent action to go into effect. Then force may be intelligently employed to subdue and disarm the recalcitrant minority.

There may be some who think I am unduly dignifying a position held by a comparatively small group by taking their arguments as seriously as I have done. But their position serves to bring into strong relief the alternatives before us. It makes clear the meaning of renascent liberalism. The alternatives are continuation of drift with attendant improvisations to meet special emergencies; dependence upon violence; dependence upon socially organized intelligence. The first two alternatives, however, are not mutually exclusive, for if things are allowed to drift the result may be some sort of social change effected by the use of force, whether so planned or not. Upon the whole, the recent policy of liberalism has been to further "social legislation"; that is, measures which add performance of social services to the older functions of government. The value of this addition is not to be despised.

It marks a decided move away from *laissez faire* liberalism, and has considerable importance in educating the public mind to a realization of the possibilities of organized social control. It has helped to develop some of the techniques that in any case will be needed in a socialized economy. But the cause of liberalism will be lost for a considerable period if it is not prepared to go further and socialize the forces of production, now at hand, so that the liberty of individuals will be supported by the very structure of economic organization.

The ultimate place of economic organization in human life is to assure the secure basis for an ordered expression of individual capacity and for the satisfaction of the needs of man in non-economic directions. The effort of mankind in connection with material production belongs, as I said earlier, among interests and activities that are, relatively speaking, routine in character, "routine" being defined as that which, without absorbing attention and energy, provides a constant basis for liberation of the values of intellectual, esthetic and companionship life. Every significant religious and moral teacher and prophet has asserted that the material is instrumental to the good life. Nominally at least, this idea is accepted by every civilized community. The transfer of the burden of material production from human muscles and brain to steam, electricity and chemical processes now makes possible the effective actualization of this ideal. Needs, wants and desires are always the moving force in generating creative action. When these wants are compelled by force of conditions to be directed for the most part, among the mass of mankind, into obtaining the means of subsistence, what should be a means becomes perforce an end in itself. Up to the present the new

mechanical forces of production, which are the means of emancipation from this state of affairs, have been employed to intensify and exaggerate the reversal of the true relation between means and ends. Humanly speaking, I do not see how it would have been possible to avoid an epoch having this character. But its perpetuation is the cause of the continually growing social chaos and strife. Its termination cannot be effected by preaching to individuals that they should place spiritual ends above material means. It can be brought about by organized social reconstruction that puts the results of the mechanism of abundance at the free disposal of individuals. The actual corrosive "materialism" of our times does not proceed from science. It springs from the notion, sedulously cultivated by the class in power, that the creative capacities of individuals can be evoked and developed only in a struggle for material possessions and material gain. We either should surrender our professed belief in the supremacy of ideal and spiritual values and accommodate our beliefs to the predominant material orientation, or we should through organized endeavor institute the socialized economy of material security and plenty that will release human energy for pursuit of higher values.

Since liberation of the capacities of individuals for free, self-initiated expression is an essential part of the creed of liberalism, liberalism that is sincere must will the means that condition the achieving of its ends. Regimentation of material and mechanical forces is the only way by which the mass of individuals can be released from regimentation and consequent suppression of their cultural possibilities. The eclipse of liberalism is due to the fact that it has not faced the alternatives and adopted the means upon which realization of its professed aims depends. Liberalism can be true to its ideals only as it takes the course that leads to their attainment. The notion that organized social control of economic forces lies outside the historic path of liberalism shows that liberalism is still impeded by remnants of its earlier *laissez faire* phase, with its opposition of society and the individual. The thing which now dampens liberal ardor and paralyzes its efforts is the conception that liberty and development of individuality as ends exclude the use of organized social effort as means. Earlier liberalism regarded the separate and competing economic action of individuals as the means to social well-being as the end. We must reverse the perspective and see that socialized economy is the means of free individual development as the end.

That liberals are divided in outlook and endeavor while reactionaries are held together by community of interests and the ties of custom is well-nigh a commonplace. Organization of standpoint and belief among liberals can be achieved only in and by unity of endeavor. Organized unity of action attended by consensus of beliefs will come about in the degree in which social control of economic forces is made the goal of liberal action. The greatest educational power, the greatest force in shaping the dispositions and attitudes of individuals, is the social medium in which they live. The medium that now lies closest to us is that of unified action for the inclusive end of a socialized economy. The attainment of a state of society in which a basis of material security will release the powers of individuals for cultural expression is not the work of a day. But by concentrating upon the task of securing a socialized economy as the ground and medium for release of the impulses and capacities

men agree to call ideal, the now scattered and often conflicting activities of liberals can be brought to effective unity.

It is no part of my task to outline in detail a program for renascent liberalism. But the question of "what is to be done" cannot be ignored. Ideas must be organized, and this organization implies an organization of individuals who hold these ideas and whose faith is ready to translate itself into action. Translation into action signifies that the general creed of liberalism be formulated as a concrete program of action. It is in organization for action that liberals are weak, and without this organization there is danger that democratic ideals may go by default. Democracy has been a fighting faith. When its ideals are reenforced by those of scientific method and experimental intelligence, it cannot be that it is incapable of evoking discipline, ardor and organization. To narrow the issue for the future to a struggle between Fascism and Communism is to invite a catastrophe that may carry civilization down in the struggle. Vital and courageous democratic liberalism is the one force that can surely avoid such a disastrous narrowing of the issue. I for one do not believe that Americans living in the tradition of Jefferson and Lincoln will weaken and give up without a wholehearted effort to make democracy a living reality. This, I repeat, involves organization.

The question cannot be answered by argument. Experimental method means experiment, and the question can be answered only by trying, by organized effort. The reasons for making the trial are not abstract or recondite. They are found in the confusion, uncertainty and conflict that mark the modern world. The reasons for thinking that the effort if made will be successful are also not abstract and remote. They lie in what the method of experimental and coöperative intelligence has already accomplished in subduing to potential human use the energies of physical nature. In material production, the method of intelligence is now the established rule; to abandon it would be to revert to savagery. The task is to go on, and not backward, until the method of intelligence and experimental control is the rule in social relations and social direction. Either we take this road or we admit that the problem of social organization in behalf of human liberty and the flowering of human capacities is insoluble.

It would be fantastic folly to ignore or to belittle the obstacles that stand in the way. But what has taken place, also against great odds, in the scientific and industrial revolutions, is an accomplished fact; the way is marked out. It may be that the way will remain untrodden. If so, the future holds the menace of confusion moving into chaos, a chaos that will be externally masked for a time by an organization of force, coercive and violent, in which the liberties of men will all but disappear. Even so, the cause of the liberty of the human spirit, the cause of opportunity of human beings for full development of their powers, the cause for which liberalism enduringly stands, is too precious and too ingrained in the human constitution to be forever obscured. Intelligence after millions of years of errancy has found itself as a method, and it will not be lost forever in the blackness of night. The business of liberalism is to bend every energy and exhibit every courage so that these precious goods may not even be temporarily lost but be intensified and expanded here and now.

Suggestions for Additional Reading

Perhaps the best introduction to the problem with which this volume is concerned is George Santayana's brilliant essay, "The Genteel Tradition in American Philosophy," in *Winds of Doctrine* (New York, 1926). A more detailed discussion of the thesis of this essay is his *Character and Opinion in the United States* (New York, 1920). Morton G. White, *Social Thought in America: The Revolt Against Formalism* (New York, 1949), treats of Dewey, Holmes, Veblen, Beard, and Robinson as a group of thinkers who together shaped the pattern of liberalism in modern America.

The most recent and comprehensive accounts of the intellectual history of the period are to be found in Merle Curti, *The Growth of American Thought* (New York, 1943); Lloyd Morris, *Postcript to Yesterday* (New York, 1947); Charles A. Beard and Mary R. Beard, *The American Spirit: A Study of the Idea of Civilization in the United States* (New York, 1942); and Ralph Henry Gabriel, *The Course of American Democratic Thought* (New York, 1940). Three other more specialized books are useful for placing pragmatism in its context: Merle Curti, *The Social Ideas of American Educators* (New York, 1935); Richard Hofstadter, *Social Darwinism in American Thought, 1860–1915* (Philadelphia, 1944); and Henry Steele Commager, *The American Mind* (New Haven, 1950).

Morris R. Cohen's article, "Later Philosophy," in *The Cambridge History of American Literature* (New York, 1921), is an excellent brief account of the philosophy of the period as a whole. For a more detailed treatment see Herbert W. Schneider, *A History of American Philosophy* (New York, 1946).

The best introduction to the writings of James and Dewey is the two volumes of selections from them in the Modern Library: Horace M. Kallen, *The Philosophy of William James* (New York, 1925), and Joseph Ratner, *John Dewey's Philosophy* (New York, 1939). A skillful and clearly written exposition of Dewey's philosophy is Sidney Hook, *John Dewey: An Intellectual Portrait* (New York: 1939).

Brief accounts of the origins of pragmatism will be found in Dewey's essay, "The Development of American Pragmatism," *Philosophy and Civilization* (New York, 1931); his intellectual autobiography, "From Absolutism to Experimentalism," *Contemporary American Philosophy*, edited by George P. Adams and W. P. Montague (2 vols., New York, 1930); and Gail Kennedy, "The Pragmatic Naturalism of Chauncey Wright," in Volume III of *Studies in the History of Ideas*, edited by the Department of Philosophy, Columbia University (New York, 1935), 477–503.

For a more adequate understanding of "pragmatism" and "instrumentalism" as theories of meaning and of truth the first and most important things to read are two essays by Charles Peirce, "The Fixation of Belief" and "How to Make Our Ideas Clear," in *Chance, Love and Logic*, ed. Morris R. Cohen (New York, 1923); chapter VI of *Pragmatism*, "Pragmatism's Conception of Truth"; Dewey's critical review of James' *Pragmatism*, "What Pragmatism Means by Practical" in his *Essays in Experimental Logic* (Chicago, 1916); and P. W. Bridgman's exposition of what he calls the "operational" theory of meaning in chapter I of his *The Logic of Modern Physics* (New York, 1928). For additional references to the extensive technical literature on this subject consult Herbert W. Schneider's *History of American Philosophy*.

Attacks on pragmatism as a philosophy of American culture will be found in Albert Schinz, *Anti-Pragmatism* (Boston, 1909); Randolph Bourne's influential essay, "Twilight of the Idols," *The Seven Arts*, II (1917), 688–700, reprinted in *Untimely Papers* (New York, 1919); Waldo Frank, *The Rediscovery of America* (New York, 1929); Van Wyck Brooks, *Three Essays on America* (New York, 1934); Mortimer J. Adler, "The Chicago School," *Harper's Magazine*, 183 (1941), 377–388; W. T. Stace, *The Destiny of Western Man* (New York, 1942); and John U. Nef, *The United States and Civilization* (Chicago, 1942).

For the defense, in addition to the books by Curti, Morris, and the Beards mentioned above, see Ralph Barton Perry, *Characteristically American* (New York, 1949); Harold Laski, *The American Democracy* (New York, 1948); Horace M. Kallen, *Individualism, An American Way of Life* (New York, 1933); and George H. Mead, "The Philosophies of Royce, James and Dewey in Their American Setting," *International Journal of Ethics*, 40 (1930), 211–231.

The best critical study of pragmatism from a Marxist point of view is V. J.

McGill, "Pragmatism Reconsidered: An Aspect of John Dewey's Philosophy," *Science and Society*, 3 (1939), 289–322. See also the comments by Corliss Lamont on this article, "John Dewey in Theory and Practice," *Science and Society*, 5 (1941), 61–64, with McGill's reply, "Further Considerations," in the same issue, 65–71, and Corliss Lamont and Howard Selsam, "Materialism and John Dewey — A Discussion," *New Masses*, 62 (February 25, 1947), 17–23. As an example of the official Russian view see the translation of an article by M. Dynnik, "Contemporary Bourgeois Philosophy in the U. S.," *Modern Review*, 1 (1947), 649–660. Two other "left-wing" criticisms of interest are Ernest Sutherland Bates, "John Dewey, America's Philosophic Engineer," *Modern Monthly*, 7 (1933), 387–396 and 404; and Benjamin Stolberg, "The Degradation of American Psychology," *Nation*, 131 (1930), 395–398.

The most detailed discussion of the pragmatic philosophy from a Catholic viewpoint is A. C. Pegis, "Man and the Challenge of Irrationalism" in *Race, Nation, Person: Social Aspects of the Race Problem*, ed. J. M. Corrigan and G. B. O'Toole (New York, 1944). Other articles by Catholics are: William O'Meara, "John Dewey and Modern Thomism," *The Thomist*, 5 (1943), 308–318; and Thomas P. Neill, "Democracy's Intellectual Fifth Column," *Catholic World*, 155 (1942), 151–155.

For the counter-attack on the many forms of anti-naturalism see the three articles by John Dewey, Sidney Hook, and Ernest Nagel in the *Partisan Review*, 10 (1943): "Anti-Naturalism in Extremis," "The New Failure of Nerve," and "Malicious Philosophies of Science." Two other trenchant replies to the anti-naturalists are Herbert Feigl, "Naturalism and Humanism," *American Quarterly*, 1

(1949), 135–148, and Sidney Hook, "Storm Signals in American Philosophy," *Virginia Quarterly Review*, 14 (1943), 29–43. In Sidney Hook, *Reason, Social Myths and Democracy* (New York, 1940), there are detailed criticisms of both the Marxist and the Thomist philosophies.

The general controversy over pragmatism and American civilization has centered around two more specific issues: the role of science, especially of the social sciences, and education. The best statement of Dewey's position on the first issue is his essay, "Science and Society," in *Philosophy and Civilization* (New York, 1931). Attacks on his thesis are: Frank H. Knight, "Pragmatism and Social Action," *International Journal of Ethics*, 46 (1936), 229–236; and Reinhold Niebuhr, *Moral Man and Immoral Society* (New York, 1932). It has been defended by Robert S. Lynd, *Knowledge for What? The Place of Social Science in American Culture* (Princeton, 1939), and George Lundberg, *Can Science Save Us?* (New York, 1947).

The debate over education has centered around Robert M. Hutchins' book, *The Higher Learning in America* (New Haven, 1936), and the "Great Books" program put into effect at St. John's College. The controversy began with a series of articles by Dewey, Hutchins, and Adler in the *Social Frontier:* "Rationality in Education," 3 (1936), 71–73, and "President Hutchins' Proposals to Remake Higher Education," 3 (1937), 103–104, by Dewey; "Grammar, Rhetoric and Mr. Dewey," 3 (1937), 137–139, by Hutchins; "The Higher Learning in America," 3 (1937), 167–169, by Dewey; and "The Crisis in Contemporary Education," 5 (1939), 140–145, by Adler. It was continued in *Fortune Magazine*. See Dewey's article, "The Challenge to Liberal Thought," *Fortune*, 30 (August, 1944); Alexander Meiklejohn, "A Reply to John Dewey," *Fortune*, 31 (January, 1945), and "A Series of Letters to the Editors of Fortune," *Fortune*, 31 (March, 1945). Hutchins also answered Dewey in "Education for Freedom," *The Christian Century*, 61 (1944), 1314–1316. There were many other contributions to this argument. Of these the most important are: Harry D. Gideonse, *The Higher Learning in a Democracy* (New York, 1937); Mortimer J. Adler, "This Pre-War Generation," *Harper's Magazine*, 181 (1940), 524–534; Sidney Hook, "The Counter-Reformation in American Education," *Antioch Review*, 1 (1941), 109–116; Alexander Meiklejohn, *Education Between Two Worlds* (New York, 1942); Mark Van Doren, *Liberal Education* (New York, 1943); and Sidney Hook, *Education for Modern Man* (New York, 1946).

The most useful bibliographies for this subject are those in Merle Curti, *The Growth of American Thought*, and Herbert W. Schneider, *A History of American Philosophy*. Ralph Barton Perry has compiled an *Annotated Bibliography of the Writings of William James* (New York, 1920), and Milton Halsey Thomas a *Bibliography of John Dewey, 1882–1939* (New York, 1939).